INVITATION TO LUKE

This volume starts a new series of commentaries specially designed to answer the need for a lively, contemporary guide to the written Word. Here is the best of contemporary biblical scholarship, together with the world-renowned Jerusalem Bible text. In addition, there are study questions that will provoke and inspire further discussion.

The Gospel of Luke was written for a church in the midst of all the problems of faith and life. Those early Christians had to wrestle with the same kind of problems that we have today. They were beset with persecution, misunderstanding, corruption, prejudice, exploitation of the poor, and social injustice.

To answer all the questions and problems, Luke wrote about a uniquely beautiful Jesus who, in fulfillment of God's promises, preaches and brings about God's rule of mercy. He gathers the sinners to him, admonishes the rich to care for the poor. Above all, Luke shows the power of prayer: Jesus always prays before important times of his life. And so should the people of his church, urges Luke. Through his Gospel, Luke presents a Jesus who consoles, guides, and challenges his people to strive to become better Christians.

Invitation to Luke presents the gospel in a format that can be easily used for individual study, daily meditation and/or group discussion. In short, it is an indispensable volume for any Christian library.

INVITATION TO LUKE

INVITATION TO LUKE

*A Commentary on the Gospel of Luke with
Complete Text from The Jerusalem Bible*

ROBERT J. KARRIS

IMAGE BOOKS
A Division of Doubleday & Company, Inc.
Garden City, New York
1977

ISBN: 0-385-12209-8
Library of Congress Catalog Card Number 77-73331
Copyright © 1977 by Robert J. Karris
All Rights Reserved
Printed in the United States of America
First Edition

In memory of my sister,
Joanne M. Pritchett
(1946–1976)

CONTENTS

General Introduction   11

Introduction   13

Luke Tells His Purpose in Writing
Luke 1:1–4   23

Jesus Is the Fulfillment of God's Promises
Luke 1:5 to 2:52   27

The Adult John and Jesus:
Jesus' Galilean Ministry
Luke 3:1 to 9:50   55

The Way to Jerusalem:
Instructions for Jesus' Followers
Luke 9:51 to 19:44   125

Jesus in Jerusalem:
Final Teaching and Rejection
Luke 19:45 to 23:56   221

The End of the Jesus Story
Is Just a Beginning
Luke 24:1–53   267

Suggested Further Readings   278

ABBREVIATIONS OF THE BOOKS
OF THE BIBLE

Ac	Acts	Lk	Luke
Am	Amos	Lm	Lamentations
Ba	Baruch	Lv	Leviticus
1 Ch	1 Chronicles	1 M	1 Maccabees
2 Ch	2 Chronicles	2 M	2 Maccabees
1 Co	1 Corinthians	Mi	Micah
2 Co	2 Corinthians	Mk	Mark
Col	Colossians	Ml	Malachi
Dn	Daniel	Mt	Matthew
Dt	Deuteronomy	Na	Nahum
Ep	Ephesians	Nb	Numbers
Est	Esther	Ne	Nehemiah
Ex	Exodus	Ob	Obadiah
Ezk	Ezekiel	1 P	1 Peter
Ezr	Ezra	2 P	2 Peter
Ga	Galatians	Ph	Philippians
Gn	Genesis	Phm	Philemon
Hab	Habakkuk	Pr	Proverbs
Heb	Hebrews	Ps	Psalms
Hg	Haggai	Qo	Ecclesiastes
Ho	Hosea	Rm	Romans
Is	Isaiah	Rt	Ruth
Jb	Job	Rv	Revelation
Jdt	Judith	1 S	1 Samuel
Jg	Judges	2 S	2 Samuel
Jl	Joel	Sg	Songs of Songs
Jm	James	Si	Ecclesiasticus
Jn	John	Tb	Tobit
1 Jn	1 John	1 Th	1 Thessalonians
2 Jn	2 John	2 Th	2 Thessalonians
3 Jn	3 John	1 Tm	1 Timothy
Jon	Jonah	2 Tm	2 Timothy
Jos	Joshua	Tt	Titus
Jr	Jeremiah	Ws	Wisdom
Jude	Jude	Zc	Zechariah
1 K	1 Kings	Zp	Zephaniah
2 K	2 Kings		

GENERAL INTRODUCTION TO
THE DOUBLEDAY NEW TESTAMENT
COMMENTARY SERIES

Let me introduce this new commentary series on the
New Testament by sharing some experiences. In my job
as New Testament Book Review Editor for the *Catholic
Biblical Quarterly,* scores of books pass through my
hands each year. As I evaluate these books and send
them out to reviewers, I cannot help but think that so
little of this scholarly research will make its way into
the hands of the educated lay person.

In talking at biblical institutes and to charismatic and
lay study groups, I find an almost unquenchable thirst
for the Word of God. People want to learn more; they
want to study. But when they ask me to recommend
commentaries on the New Testament, I'm stumped.
What commentaries can I put into their hands, commentaries that do not have the technical jargon of
scholars and really communicate to the educated laity?

The goal of this popular commentary series is to
make the best of contemporary scholarship available to
the educated lay person in a highly readable and understandable way. The commentaries avoid footnotes and
other scholarly apparatus. They are short and sweet.
The authors make their points in a clear way and don't
fatigue their readers with unnecessary detail.

Another outstanding feature of this commentary
series is that it is based on the Jerusalem Bible translation, which is serialized with the commentary. This
lively and easily understandable translation has received

rave reviews from millions of readers. It is the interstate of translations and avoids the stop lights of local-road translations.

A signal feature of the commentaries on the Gospels is that they explore the way each evangelist used the sayings and deeds of Jesus to meet the needs of his church. The commentators answer the question: How did each evangelist guide, challenge, teach, and console the members of his community with the message of Jesus? The commentators are not interested in the evangelist's message for its own sake, but explain that message with one eye on present application.

This last-mentioned feature goes hand and glove with the innovative feature of appending Study Questions to the explanations of individual passages. By means of these Study Questions the commentator moves from an explanation of the message of the evangelist to a consideration of how this message might apply to believers today.

Each commentator has two highly important qualifications: scholarly expertise and the proven ability to communicate the results of solid scholarship to the people of God.

I am confident that this new commentary series will meet a real need as it helps people to unlock a door to the storehouse of God's Word where they will find food for life.

ROBERT J. KARRIS, O.F.M.
Associate Professor of New Testament Studies,
Catholic Theological Union and
Chicago Cluster of Theological Schools

INTRODUCTION

In this Introduction I'd like to invite my readers to engage in an exercise of imagination. Visualize with me the situation of Luke and his church around A.D. 75. The images you conjure up and store in your memory will greatly help you to appreciate the messages Luke addresses to his community.

LUKE'S HOME IS A MISSIONARY CENTER

Luke's home is a missionary center from which the church sends missionaries to Jewish and pagan peoples. It may be convenient for my readers to imagine a contemporary missionary center. From it the apostolic tradition goes forth and comes into contact and conflict with different cultures. Important questions begin to pop up all over the place. How much can the Christian message be adapted to a new culture without its being compromised? Can we use the native language and architectural style in liturgy? How can we teach monogamous marriage? How can we continue to preach in that region since the government has imprisoned some of our missionaries? In other words, we should not imagine the missionary center for which Luke wrote as existing on some balmy, tranquil island, isolated from the problems of faith and life. That missionary center throbbed with the many problems of making the Christian message alive for different peoples and cultures.

THE TRIALS OF MISSIONARY WORK

From the little we have said about Luke's home as a missionary center, it is somewhat easy to imagine the ups and downs his community experienced on mission. There were peaceful missions, but most often there were turbulent missions. Some of this turbulence is reflected in the new admonitions Jesus gives his disciples after the Last Supper: " 'When I sent you out without purse or haversack or sandals, were you short of anything?' 'No,' they said. He said to them, 'But now if you have a purse, take it; if you have a haversack, do the same; if you have no sword, sell your cloak and buy one' " (Lk 22:35–36). The Acts of the Apostles are replete with the trials of a missionary like Paul: "Then some Jews arrived from Antioch and Iconium, and turned the people against the apostles. They stoned Paul and dragged him outside the town, thinking he was dead. . . . [The apostles] put fresh heart into the disciples, encouraging them to persevere in the faith. 'We all have to experience many hardships,' they said, 'before we enter the kingdom of God' " (Ac 14:19, 22).

PERSECUTION

As the last-cited quotation from the Acts of the Apostles and frequent passages in the Gospel show, Luke's church was experiencing persecution both in the missionary field and at home. We should not imagine this persecution as the throw-them-to-the-lions type. It was sporadic, unofficial persecution from both Jewish and Gentile fronts. This is a type of persecution we have become familiar with as we read of the accounts of what is happening to Christians in some parts of Latin America: One day people see you as a champion of the cause of the oppressed; the next day you're not around; the day after you're seen again but all the fight has been beaten out of you. It's the persecution of verbal abuse, the persecution of economic boycotts and reprisals. "You may have a nice tailor shop going, but we won't buy from you nor sell you cloth. Try to make ends meet." "You want your son to learn how to make shoes? Well, we won't take him in as an apprentice." Or the Christians might flee their homes on the rumor of persecution to join together with their fellow Christians in another ward of the city, only to find people looting the homes they had vacated.

MERCY TO THE OUTCASTS AND TO REPENTANT APOSTATES

As members of Luke's church embarked on mission, some were tempted to fudge about the mercy of the Messiah under whose banner they traveled. People of different cultures might seem so helplessly perverse that Jesus' message of God's mercy surely couldn't be for them. These people might be imagined as people who valued their herds of livestock more than the lives of their children and for whom stealing was a way of life. God's mercy is for them, Luke insists, as he recounts story after story and saying after saying of how Jesus befriended the outcasts and sinners.

Trapped in situations where persecution was not a nice word from the hoary past but a real drain on one's faith and life, a few Christians of Luke's time escaped the trap by throwing in the towel on their faith. But after a time, some of them repented. Could and should the church take these people back into their ranks? Luke, with such teachings as Jesus' incomparable parable of the Prodigal Son, gives a positive answer to this faith-clattering question.

THE PROBLEMS OF THE RICH CHRISTIANS

Luke ranks high in the popular esteem as the champion of the poor. More aptly, he might be called the conscience of the rich. Imagine Luke as well educated, as at home in both the Jewish and Greco-Roman cultures as a son of missionary parents. He was quick to spot the problems which rich Christians were creating for his community. Bred in the Greco-Roman culture which had almost no concern for the poor, these rich folk had great difficulty adapting Jesus' teaching on care for the poor. The effort needed to shake off this cultural conditioning reached heroic proportions when these rich Christians realized that their full allegiance to the Christian message might cost them their possessions in times of persecution. Some of these rich folk may have called in outside consultants who reassured them that their wealth was a sign of God's favor and that they should not get guilt feelings over not helping the poor and over absenting themselves from the Christian roll call on the eve of persecution.

LESS-THAN-EXEMPLARY CHURCH LEADERS

As the recent history of the United States so amply shows, corruption can reach to high places. Luke's community had a taste of that experience. It was so easy for some of its leaders to adopt the cultural standards of pagan leaders and use their positions not for the furthering of God's kingdom but for the feathering of their own nests. Instead of excelling as servants of others, some church leaders excelled in their demands for champagne service. Instead of using the church's money to aid the poor, some used it to buy more stock in the good life.

LUKE WRITES AFTER THE DESTRUCTION OF JERUSALEM

We have often enough heard from pulpits that the destruction of Jerusalem and its Temple were important events for the early Christians. Yet I would venture that we have infrequently imagined ourselves back into that situation of A.D. 70. Imagine the annihilation of Rome and the Vatican; imagine that no-trespassing signs forbade Catholics from entering the area and undertaking any reconstruction. What would happen to the papacy? With their central headquarters destroyed, how would Catholics maintain unity throughout the world? Who would lead and teach and instruct them? No doubt, some self-appointed prophets would arise to trumpet that such annihilation signaled the end of the world. Others would turn up the volume of anxiety by proclaiming that this destruction surely spells the end of Catholicism. The emotions which would pulse through Roman Catholics at the mere prospect of Rome and the Vatican being obliterated are quite similar to those which coursed through the members of Luke's community when Jerusalem and its Temple were razed in A.D. 70. It was not as if some far-off city like Taipei had been liquidated. One's hometown and the symbol of one's religious heritage had been leveled.

WHEN IS THE LORD JESUS COMING?

The destruction of Jerusalem and its Temple had broad repercussions in the Lukan communities. Was such havoc a sure sign that the faithful Lord was coming in judgment, was coming to rescue his persecuted church from its struggles? Luke consoles his community that the Lord is surely coming. But since nobody knows the when of that coming, Jerusalem's destruction cannot be a sign that his coming is just around the corner. Luke gives his communities great solace by reminding them that the God whose rule Jesus brought about is a merciful and gracious God. When his Son does come, he will be as merciful and gracious.

GOD'S FIDELITY TO HIS PROMISES TO THE JEWISH PEOPLE

The destruction of Jerusalem and its Temple may have caused many a Christian to ask the question: Is God really faithful to his promises? If he were so faithful, why did he let Jerusalem and its Temple—those signs of his presence and care for his people—be razed to the ground? To these perplexing questions Luke insists that God has been faithful to the promises he made to the Jewish people. While the religious leaders rejected God's Messiah, Jesus, some of the Jewish rank and file heeded Jesus' message. The Christian people is built upon those Jews who accepted God's fulfillment of his promises in the Messiah, Jesus. The destruction of Jerusalem and its Temple is God's judgment on the infidelity of the religious leaders.

FALSE TEACHERS

There were some false teachers on the prowl in the Lukan communities who disturbed the people with announcements that the destruction of Jerusalem and its Temple are sure signs that the Lord is about to come in judgment for all peoples. Other false teachers, who despised the body, maintained that the bodily resurrection of Jesus was nonsense. Luke's Paul had foreseen the trouble such false teachers would create for the churches when he advised the Ephesian elders: "I know quite well that when I have gone fierce wolves will invade you and will have no mercy on the flock. Even from your own ranks there will be men coming forward with a travesty of the truth on their lips to induce the disciples to follow them" (Ac 20:29–30).

JESUS, GOD'S MESSAGE OF MERCY

All the points I have mentioned so far come together in the uniquely beautiful picture which Luke has painted of Jesus the Messiah. Jesus is the missionary par excellence who, in fulfillment of God's promises, preaches and brings about God's rule of mercy. He embraces the outcasts and sinners with the arms of God's mercy and admonishes the rich to care for the poor. As the model servant, he instructs his disciples in the fine art of dying to self to serve others. Opposition and rejection hound his every step to the crucifixion. He dies as an innocent martyr, confident that God will be true to his promises and not abandon him. His hope is not disappointed. As Risen Lord, he becomes the one in whose name repentance for the forgiveness of sins is preached to all the nations.

LUKE AND US

We have come to the conclusion of this Introduction. My readers may say that they have found my exercise in imagination interesting, but somewhat quaint. They muse that Luke's situation is light-years away from their experience today. Is it? Today, in an age of religious future shock we are struggling with the "missionary" questions of how much is revelation and how much is cultural baggage? What are the roles of women? Should they be ordained? Is homosexuality wrong? The problem of the haves and have-nots is still with us today even though it is dressed up in technological and Third World clothing. What about persecution and discrimination in parts of the United States, in Poland, in Lithuania, in Latin America? What about the cries one hears from the right that there are termites gnawing away at the bark of the church? What about the cries that we should not share the table fellowship of the Eucharist with divorced Christians? Cries that we should not show mercy to those chocolate soldiers in the army of Christ who melted with the first heat of opposition and conflict? How different are the problems we face today from those which the Christians of Luke's time faced? We may be taller, heavier, and more sharply dressed than the Christians of Luke's day, but we have the same problems and the same quest—the quest to make the message of Jesus Christ vibrate in our lives in a changed situation.

LUKE THE GOOD PASTOR

We have imagined ourselves in Luke's situation and glimpsed how similar our situation is. But what did Luke do in his situation? He used the sources of Christian tradition available to him—Mark's Gospel, collections of Jesus' sayings common to his Gospel and Matthew's, and his own church's traditions—to answer the faith questions of his communities. In consoling, guiding, and challenging them, he is not like some university professor who authors a dogmatics which treats all Christian problems from A to Z. He is more like a good pastor who creatively adapts the Christian message to speak to the needs of his people. He tells them that just as Jesus showed mercy to the despised tax collectors of his time, so too must they extend mercy to the despised peoples they meet. Just as Jesus confronted the Pharisees of his day for their legalism, so too must they confront those in their church who equate love of God and neighbor with the observance of so many rituals. It is a sign of the effectiveness of Luke's pastoring that his Gospel continues to speak so eloquently to both pastors and parishioners today. (See the commentary on Lk 1:1–4 for more detail.)

ACKNOWLEDGMENTS

The format of this popular commentary precludes those scholarly indicators of acknowledgment—footnotes. My colleagues in the biblical guild will easily spot the opinions of those scholars upon whose work I have built. I would like to single out for special mention the work of the Belgian Benedictine Dom Jacques Dupont.

Besides being a Lukan scholar without peer, he has been a skillful teacher, challenging me to think and evaluate things anew. He has been a most faith-filled pastor, sensitizing me to the relevance of Luke's message for our times and problems.

I would also like to acknowledge the debt of gratitude I owe to Ms. Shirley Brin for the most careful work she did in preparing this manuscript for publication.

DEDICATION

I dedicate this commentary to the memory of my only sister, Joanne M. Pritchett, who bore her terminal cancer with calm fortitude and cared more for others than for herself. "Anyone who tries to preserve her life will lose it; and anyone who loses it will keep it safe" (Lk 17:33).

Luke Tells His Purpose in Writing
Luke 1:1–4

Luke 1:1-4
LUKE TELLS HIS PURPOSE
IN WRITING

¹ 1 Seeing that many others have undertaken to
  draw up accounts of the events that have taken
² place among us, ·exactly as these were handed
  down to us by those who from the outset were eye-
³ witnesses and ministers of the word, ·I in my turn,
  after carefully going over the whole story from the
  beginning, have decided to write an ordered ac-
⁴ count for you, Theophilus, ·so that your Excellency
  may learn how well founded the teaching is that
  you have received.

✠

This majestic, four-verse sentence is like the preface
of a book. In it Luke states his purpose for writing both
his Gospel and the Acts of the Apostles. In verses 1
and 2 he emphasizes that the tradition he incorporates
into his work is apostolic—that is, tradition which stems
from the eyewitnesses and preachers of the word. In
verses 3 and 4 he tells the Theophiluses of his church
why he is writing a new account—an account which will
supplement Mark's Gospel. Uppermost in his mind is
the intention of showing the Theophiluses "how well
founded" their instruction is. That teaching is well
founded because it is not a fly-by-night operation. It
is well founded because, like a strong bank or government, it inspires confidence in Theophilus today. Put
in other ways, Luke is not primarily concerned with

showing Theophilus that his contemporary faith is well founded because a dozen sayings of Jesus from apostolic tradition support a particular point of that faith. Nor does Luke deal with apostolic tradition like some museum curator who is charged with cataloguing ancient artifacts for a new generation of Theophiluses. He is more like a good pastor who preaches the ancient truths of the faith with such conviction that he instills renewed confidence in his people, who makes the Christian tradition speak a powerful word of consolation to the bereaved, and who makes the time-honored message of God's mercy so palpably present to those seized by anxiety that it sparks new hope in them.

As we have noted in the Introduction, Luke is very much concerned with contemporary problems within his church. He strives by might and main to build up Theophilus's confidence in the apostolic tradition, a confidence which is being shaken by circumstances all around him: persecution, the trials of missionary work, false teachers, less-than-exemplary church leaders, the problems of rich folk. Underlying all Theophilus's problems, tensions, and sleepless nights are the questions: Is God merciful and gracious? Is he faithful to his promises? In the commentary on the rest of the Gospel we will have multiple occasions to see how Luke inspires and assures the Theophiluses of his church that their faith is indeed well founded.

Jesus Is the Fulfillment of God's Promises
Luke 1:5 to 2:52

Introduction to Luke 1:5 to 2:52
JESUS IS THE FULFILLMENT OF GOD'S PROMISES

A woman recently shared a priceless discovery with me. As she beamed with the happiness of her find, she confided to me that by reading through the first two chapters of Luke's Gospel in one sitting she had chanced upon treasure after treasure which she never knew existed. Before she had hit it rich in the treasure land of these chapters, she thought she had a good hold on the meaning of the Christmas story. But now she viewed Mary, the angels, the shepherds, and the infant lying in the manger in the floodlight of the rest of these two chapters. Before you read the commentary on these first chapters, both she and I would highly recommend that you read these two chapters in one sitting. Let the entire sweep of the story fill the horizons of your understanding. You, too, will share the joy of discovering the riches of Luke's story. In the remaining paragraphs of this introduction I will give you some handy hints on what to look for.

As you read through these chapters, you will quickly spy Luke, the consummate artist at work. He is a master with parallelisms. The annunciation of John the Baptist's birth (1:5–25) is parallel to the annunciation of Jesus' birth (1:26–38). The response of one mother-to-be, Elizabeth (1:39–45) is parallel to the response of the other mother-to-be, Mary (1:46–55). The birth of John the Baptist (1:57–58) is parallel to the birth

of Jesus (2:1–20). The circumcision and naming of
John the Baptist (1:59–79) are parallel to those of Jesus (2:21). Luke does not deal in parallelisms just to
doll up his story. The parallelisms are his vehicles of
theological freight as he contrasts John the Baptist
with Jesus. In each instance Jesus is greater. For example, John the Baptist "will be great in the sight of
the Lord" (1:15), whereas Jesus "will be great and will
be called Son of the Most High" (1:32). The door to
one of the treasures of meaning in these chapters can
be unlocked by reading Luke's parallelisms carefully.

If we ask ourselves about Luke's purpose in these
chapters, we are put on the track of uncovering their
most valuable treasure. These chapters not only reveal
who Jesus is, but also show how one must respond to
that revelation—in joyful confession. At the very beginning of his gospel story Luke wants to make it crystal
clear to his readers who Jesus is. Jesus is the fulfillment
of God's promises in the Old Testament, the Son of
God, the Savior, the Christ of the Lord, the one who
is destined for the fall and rise of many in Israel. The
story that unfolds in the remainder of the Gospel
is about this Jesus. Mary, Zechariah, the shepherds,
Simeon, and Anna confess their faith in God and joyfully sing the praises of him who acted in Jesus for humankind's salvation.

There is another side to the coin of Luke's purpose.
He uses these chapters as a theological overture to the
themes he will orchestrate in the rest of his Gospel and
in the Acts of the Apostles. What has happened at Jesus' birth is the result of God's fulfillment of his promises. As Mary sings, "He has come to the help of Israel
his servant, mindful of his mercy—*according to the
promise* he made to our ancestors—of his mercy to
Abraham and to his descendants for ever" (1:54–55).

The Gospel will end (24:6–7, 25–27, 44–45) and the Acts of the Apostles will begin (1:4) on that very same note. Zechariah, Mary, the shepherds, Simeon, and Anna are types of those who wait expectantly for God to fulfill his promise of mercy. Note the description of the prophetess Anna: "she spoke of the child to all *who looked forward to the deliverance of Jerusalem*" (2:38). This theme is picked up in the gospel injunctions to pray continually and never lose heart even though God seems to be asleep and disinterested in fulfilling his promises (see 18:1–8). It is no mere happenstance that the Gospel opens with a scene in the Temple (1:5–25; see also 2:22–52) and ends with the disciples "continually in the Temple praising God" (24:53). Nor that the Acts of the Apostles describes the early Christian community as going "as a body to the Temple every day" (Ac 2:46). Jesus and the Christian movement are not born on some desert island, but in the land of God's promises. They are heirs to those promises symbolized by God's presence in the Temple. That God's message is readily accepted by the lowly and outcast like Mary and the shepherds will form a prominent theme in the Gospel, where Jesus is depicted as associating freely with people of that sort (see 15:1–2). Although space prevents us from detailing additional themes, enough has been said to show that this section is truly an overture to Luke's Gospel. Keeping in mind the handy hint that Luke's primary purpose in this section is to proclaim who Jesus is, not to share vignettes from Mary's family album, will help the reader amass treasures of unsurpassing worth.

The last handy hint I proffer is a plea for perseverance in the pursuit of the wealth of these chapters, for you are going to encounter one obstacle or another on the way. Perhaps the biggest obstacle is that the traditions which Luke has joined together by means of his artistic parallelisms are not of the same kind. Put another way, the different traditions do not employ the same theological language to express who Jesus is. For example, the traditions behind chapter 2 do not seem to be aware of the annunciation to Mary and her virginal conception. In verses 27, 33, 41, and 48 of chapter 2 we read of Jesus' father and mother. Despite what chapter 1 says about the angel Gabriel's annunciation of Jesus' sonship with God, Mary does not understand that Jesus must be busy with his Father's affairs (2:50). Although she has been made privy to Jesus' status as Son of God, Mary ponders the meaning of the shepherds' message (2:19) and of the child Jesus' answer (2:51) as if both were new revelations about the nature of her son. In the commentary proper we will help the reader persevere through and overcome these obstacles to unearthing the treasures of these chapters.

Luke 1:5–38
THE PARALLEL ANNUNCIATIONS

5   In the days of King Herod of Judaea there lived
a priest called Zechariah who belonged to the
Abijah section of the priesthood, and he had a
wife, Elizabeth by name, who was a descendant
6 of Aaron. ·Both were worthy in the sight of God,
and scrupulously observed all the commandments
7 and observances of the Lord. ·But they were child-
less: Elizabeth was barren and they were both getting on in years.

8   Now it was the turn of Zechariah's section to
serve, and he was exercising his priestly office be-
9 fore God ·when it fell to him by lot, as the ritual
custom was, to enter the Lord's sanctuary and
10 burn incense there. ·And at the hour of incense
the whole congregation was outside, praying.

11   Then there appeared to him the angel of the
Lord, standing on the right of the altar of incense.
12 The sight disturbed Zechariah and he was over-
13 come with fear. ·But the angel said to him, "Zechariah, do not be afraid, your prayer has been
heard. Your wife Elizabeth is to bear you a son
14 and you must name him John. ·He will be your
joy and delight and many will rejoice at his birth,
15 for he will be great in the sight of the Lord; he
must drink no wine, no strong drink. Even from
his mother's womb he will be filled with the Holy
16 Spirit, ·and he will bring back many of the sons
17 of Israel to the Lord their God. ·With the spirit
and power of Elijah, he will go before him to
turn the hearts of fathers toward their children
and the disobedient back to the wisdom that the
virtuous have, preparing for the Lord a people fit
18 for him." ·Zechariah said to the angel, "How can

I be sure of this? I am an old man and my wife
19 is getting on in years." ·The angel replied, "I am
Gabriel who stand in God's presence, and I have
been sent to you and bring you this good news.
20 Listen! Since you have not believed my words,
which will come true at their appointed time, you
will be silenced and have no power of speech
21 until this has happened." ·Meanwhile the people
were waiting for Zechariah and were surprised
22 that he stayed in the sanctuary so long. ·When he
came out he could not speak to them, and they
realized that he had received a vision in the sanctuary. But he could only make signs to them, and
remained dumb.
23   When his time of service came to an end he
24 returned home. ·Some time later his wife Elizabeth conceived, and for five months she kept to
25 herself. ·"The Lord has done this for me," she
said, "now that it has pleased him to take away
the humiliation I suffered among men."
26   In the sixth month the angel Gabriel was sent
27 by God to a town in Galilee called Nazareth, ·to
a virgin betrothed to a man named Joseph, of the
House of David; and the virgin's name was Mary.
28 He went in and said to her, "Rejoice, so highly
29 favored! The Lord is with you." ·She was deeply
disturbed by these words and asked herself what
30 this greeting could mean, ·but the angel said to
her, "Mary, do not be afraid; you have won God's
31 favor. ·Listen! You are to conceive and bear a
32 son, and you must name him Jesus. ·He will be
great and will be called Son of the Most High.
The Lord God will give him the throne of his an-
33 cestor David; ·he will rule over the House of Jacob
34 for ever and his reign will have no end." ·Mary
said to the angel, "But how can this come about,
35 since I am a virgin?" ·"The Holy Spirit will come
upon you," the angel answered, "and the power
of the Most High will cover you with its shadow.
And so the child will be holy and will be called
36 Son of God. ·Know this too: your kinswoman
Elizabeth has, in her old age, herself conceived

a son, and she whom people called barren is now
37 in her sixth month, ·for nothing is impossible to
38 God." ·"I am the handmaid of the Lord," said
Mary, "let what you have said be done to me."
And the angel left her.

✠

The annunciations of the births of John the Baptist
and Jesus follow a stereotype Old Testament pattern
about the birth of a notable figure in salvation history.
This pattern, evidenced for example in the story of the
birth of Isaac (see Gn 17:1, 3, 15–16, 17, 19), has
five points:

1. An angel or God appears (see Lk 1:11 and
   1:26);
2. the recipient of the announcement is
   troubled (see 1:12 and 1:29);
3. reassurance is given and the birth is announced (see 1:13–17 and 1:30–31);
4. the recipient of the announcement raises an
   objection (see 1:18 and 1:34);
5. a sign is given to confirm the birth (see
   1:19–20 and 1:36–37).

As you study the annunciation to Mary, you will
note how closely it corresponds to the Old Testament
pattern except in verses 32–33, 35, and 38, which ex-
pand the pattern much as you might develop the basic
pattern of a letter to a friend by adding your own personal touch. These verses convey the import of Jesus'
and Mary's significance in salvation history. The first
expansion, in verses 32–33, clearly resonates with the
promise God made to David through the prophet

Nathan, a promise which became a cornerstone of messianic expectation: "Yahweh will make you great. I will make his royal throne secure for ever. I will be a father to him and he a son to me. Your House and your sovereignty will always stand secure before me and your throne be established for ever" (2 S 7:11, 13, 14, 16). Jesus, of the house of David, is the fulfillment of God's promise to David, his ancient forefather. But Jesus is more, as the second expansion, in verse 35, proclaims. Jesus is Son of God at his conception. The third expansion, in verse 38, highlights Mary as the model of staunch faith. Later on Elizabeth will bless Mary "who believed that the promise made her by the Lord would be fulfilled" (1:45).

As we mentioned earlier, in the introduction to chapters 1 and 2, the tradition embodied in the annunciation to Mary stands in tension with traditions in chapter 2. It also stands in tension with other traditions in the New Testament, such as Romans 1:3-4, which teaches that Jesus was declared God's Son at his resurrection, and Mark 1:11, which teaches that Jesus was declared God's Son at his baptism. Its teaching of Mary's virginal conception also stands in tension with the earlier New Testament writings (e.g., Paul's epistles), which are silent on this vital matter. Once one is aware of these tensions, how does one relieve them? They cannot be swept under the carpet. The tensions do not result from a change in Jesus' nature, as if divine sonship, bestowed on him at his resurrection, somehow became retroactive for his baptism and conception. No, the tensions stem from changes in understanding the reality which was Jesus' from the first. Jesus was Son of God not only at his resurrection and baptism, but also at his conception. Jesus' virginal conception (1:35) relates to this fuller understanding of Jesus and underlines his origin in God.

STUDY QUESTION: This section portrays Jesus' place in God's plan for salvation. How does Jesus figure in our plan for salvation?

Luke 1:39–56
THE TWO MOTHERS-TO-BE

39 Mary set out at that time and went as quickly as she could to a town in the hill country of Judah.
40 She went into Zechariah's house and greeted Eliz-
41 abeth. ·Now as soon as Elizabeth heard Mary's greeting, the child leaped in her womb and Eliza-
42 beth was filled with the Holy Spirit. ·She gave a loud cry and said, "Of all women you are the most blessed, and blessed is the fruit of your
43 womb. ·Why should I be honored with a visit from
44 the mother of my Lord? ·For the moment your greeting reached my ears, the child in my womb
45 leaped for joy. ·Yes, blessed is she who believed that the promise made her by the Lord would be fulfilled."
46 And Mary said:

"My soul proclaims the greatness of the Lord
47 and my spirit *exults in God my savior;*
48 because *he has looked upon his lowly handmaid.*
Yes, from this day forward all generations will call me blessed,
49 for the Almighty has done great things for me.
Holy is his name,
50 and *his mercy reaches from age to age for those who fear him.*
51 He has shown the power of his arm,
he has routed the proud of heart.
52 *He has pulled down princes* from their thrones *and exalted the lowly.*
53 *The hungry he has filled with good things,* the rich sent empty away.

54 *He has come to the help of Israel his servant,*
        mindful of his mercy
55 —according to the promise he made to our an-
        cestors—
      of his mercy to Abraham and to his descend-
        ants for ever."

56 Mary stayed with Elizabeth about three months
    and then went back home.

✠

Mary's Magnificat (1:46–55), the first of four canti-
cles which Luke sets in these chapters, is like a song
in a musical play. Such a song, like "Tradition" in
Fiddler on the Roof, does not interrupt the movement
of the story as much as it interprets what has just happened.

An analysis of Mary's song will help us appreciate
its interpretation of Jesus' conception by a lowly handmaid. Its two stanzas are verses 46–50 and 51–55.
Verses 49b–50 and 54b–55 correspond to one another
in terminology and signal the end of their respective
stanzas:

"Holy is his name,
and *his mercy* reaches from age to age for those who
    fear him" (1:49b–50).

"mindful of *his mercy*
—according to the promise he made to our ancestors—
of *his mercy* to Abraham and to his descendants for
    ever" (1:54b–55).

In the first stanza God's beneficence toward Mary,
the lowly maiden, is clearly in the forefront. Because
of what God has done for her, she will be blessed by

all future generations. At the end of the first stanza the
perspective of the song broadens as it ranges from
God's mercy to this particular woman to God's mercy
from age to age to "those who fear him" (1:50).
Verses 54b–55, which correspond to verses 49b–50, interpret that broadened perspective within God's plan of
salvation: Jesus is God's act of mercy which fulfills the
promise God gave to Abraham at the beginning of salvation history.

The second stanza introduces a tension into the
movement of the song. God's act is not just mercy for
the lowly Mary; it also spells the overthrow of the
proud, mighty, and rich. But it is palpably obvious that
the conception of Jesus did not result in the overthrow
of such people. This tension is due to the fact that songs
are fabled for dreaming dreams and seeing visions.
God's concern for the humble Mary becomes a sign of
his concern for the lowly of all ages. Put another way,
the role of Jesus is to continue God's mercy toward the
lowly by overthrowing their oppressors.

The song strives mightily to interpret the event of
the Son of God's conception by a lowly woman. Jesus,
the fulfillment of God's promise of mercy, serves as a
sign of God's fidelity to his promises. God's action for
the lowly handmaid Mary presents a dramatic vision
of what salvation is all about. In the end, the lowly will
be exalted, and the proud routed.

As the Gospel unfolds, we will have occasion time
and again to highlight both Luke's picture of Jesus,
savior of the lowly, and Luke's concern for his persecuted Christians who in their lowliness and hunger hope
vigorously that God will be faithful to his promise to
save them from their oppressors.

STUDY QUESTIONS: The song sings of the powerful and lowly. Who are the powerful and lowly of our time? Into what category do we fit?

Luke 1:57-80
THE BIRTH, CIRCUMCISION, AND NAMING OF JOHN

⁵⁷ Meanwhile the time came for Elizabeth to have
⁵⁸ her child, and she gave birth to a son; ·and when
her neighbors and relations heard that the Lord
had shown her so great a kindness, they shared
her joy.

⁵⁹ Now on the eighth day they came to circum-
cise the child; they were going to call him Zecha-
⁶⁰ riah after his father, ·but his mother spoke up.
⁶¹ "No," she said, "he is to be called John." ·They
said to her, "But no one in your family has that
⁶² name," ·and made signs to his father to find out
⁶³ what he wanted him called. ·The father asked for
a writing tablet and wrote, "His name is John."
⁶⁴ And they were all astonished. ·At that instant
his power of speech returned and he spoke and
⁶⁵ praised God. ·All their neighbors were filled with
awe and the whole affair was talked about
⁶⁶ throughout the hill country of Judaea. ·All those
who heard of it treasured it in their hearts. "What
will this child turn out to be?" they wondered.
And indeed the hand of the Lord was with him.
⁶⁷ His father Zechariah was filled with the Holy
Spirit and spoke this prophecy:

⁶⁸ *"Blessed be the Lord, the God of Israel,*
for he has visited his people, he has come to
their rescue
⁶⁹ and he has raised up for us a power for salvation
in the House of his servant David,
⁷⁰ even as he proclaimed,
by the mouth of his holy prophets from ancient times,

71   that he would save us from our enemies
     and from the hands of all who hate us.

72   Thus he shows mercy to our ancestors,
     thus *he remembers* his holy *covenant,*

73   the oath he swore
     to our father Abraham

74   that he would grant us, free from fear,
     to be delivered from the hands of our enemies,

75   to serve him in holiness and virtue
     in his presence, all our days.

76   And you, little child,
     you shall be called Prophet of the Most High,
     for you will go before the Lord
     to prepare the way for him.

77   To give his people knowledge of salvation
     through the forgiveness of their sins;

78   this by the tender mercy of our God
     who from on high will bring the rising Sun to
       visit us,

79   to give light to *those who live*
     in darkness and the shadow of death,
     and to guide our feet
     into the way of peace."

80   Meanwhile the child grew up and his spirit matured. And he lived out in the wilderness until the day he appeared openly to Israel.

✠

Just as Mary's Magnificat interpreted God's gift of Jesus, so too does Zechariah's canticle—the Benedictus (1:67–79)—interpret God's gift to him of his son, John.

Luke's introduction to the Benedictus pictures Zechariah, filled with the Holy Spirit and prophesying. As the messianic age dawns in the birth of Jesus, God renews his gift of prophecy. His prophets—Zechariah, Simeon, and Anna—proclaim the meaning of God's greatest act of mercy—Jesus. The spirit of prophecy will also characterize the birth of the Christian Church, as detailed in Acts 1–2.

The Benedictus itself is composed of two stanzas, verses 68–75 and 76–79, and utilizes biblical terms and images. (The biblical terms and images are italicized in the text of the Benedictus; see also the italicized words in Mary's Magnificat.) In the first stanza Zechariah blesses God, who, in acting in mercy and fulfilling his promise to Abraham, has visited his people in Jesus. God has determined to come to the rescue of his people by subduing any force which instills fear in his people (1:74). In doing this, God intends that his people serve him in holiness and virtue all their days (1:75).

The second stanza echoes the description of John's role as outlined by the angel Gabriel in 1:16–17. Again God's mercy is emphasized (1:78). The rescue which John will proclaim and defend is not nationalistic sovereignty, but forgiveness of sins, the light of life, and peace.

STUDY QUESTION: Who exactly is John that Luke stops the action of his narrative to dedicate a song to him?

Luke 2:1–21
THE BIRTH, CIRCUMCISION,
AND NAMING OF JESUS

1 2 Now at this time Caesar Augustus issued a decree for a census of the whole world to be 2 taken. ·This census—the first—took place while 3 Quirinius was governor of Syria, ·and everyone 4 went to his own town to be registered. ·So Joseph set out from the town of Nazareth in Galilee and traveled up to Judaea, to the town of David called Bethlehem, since he was of David's House and 5 line, ·in order to be registered together with Mary, 6 his betrothed, who was with child. ·While they were there the time came for her to have her 7 child, ·and she gave birth to a son, her first-born. She wrapped him in swaddling clothes, and laid him in a manger because there was no room for 8 them at the inn. ·In the countryside close by there were shepherds who lived in the fields and took it in turns to watch their flocks during the night. 9 The angel of the Lord appeared to them and the glory of the Lord shone around them. They were 10 terrified, ·but the angel said, "Do not be afraid. Listen, I bring you news of great joy, a joy to be 11 shared by the whole people. ·Today in the town of David a savior has been born to you; he is 12 Christ the Lord. ·And here is a sign for you: you will find a baby wrapped in swaddling clothes and 13 lying in a manger." ·And suddenly with the angel there was a great throng of the heavenly host, praising God and singing:

14   "Glory to God in the highest heaven,
         and peace to men who enjoy his favor."

15 Now when the angels had gone from them into heaven, the shepherds said to one another, "Let us go to Bethlehem and see this thing that has happened which the Lord has made known to 16 us." ·So they hurried away and found Mary and 17 Joseph, and the baby lying in the manger. ·When they saw the child they repeated what they had 18 been told about him, ·and everyone who heard it was astonished at what the shepherds had to say. 19 As for Mary, she treasured all these things and 20 pondered them in her heart. ·And the shepherds went back glorifying and praising God for all they had heard and seen; it was exactly as they had been told.

21 When the eighth day came and the child was to be circumcised, they gave him the name Jesus, the name the angel had given him before his conception.

✠

Its great influence on Christmas crib scenes and on the selection of the Gospel read at Christmas services has imprinted Luke's account of Jesus' birth on the minds and hearts of millions of Christians. Christmas sermon after sermon has deepened that imprint. In what follows we will emboss that imprint by pointing out the rich scriptural meditation behind the tradition which Luke preserves in this section. We divide the section into four parts.

THE SETTING OF JESUS' BIRTH

2:1–7 While setting the stage for the angels' revelation, which is the heart of 2:1–21, verses 1–7 make some profound statements of their own about Jesus. Luke introduces Caesar Augustus and his worldwide census not only to spotlight Jesus' birth as signally important within the flow of universal human history, but also to teach that Jesus brings the peace for which Augustus was renowned. Far from being an innocuous counting of noses, the census was a scheme hatched to raise more tax revenue. Although others may have revolted against the Roman rule which enforced census-taking, Joseph, like Jesus and his followers later on, is obedient to Roman rule and journeys to Bethlehem from Nazareth for the census. This census also provides Luke with a means of telling how Jesus was born in Bethlehem in fulfillment of the prophecies of his birth. In Matthew's Gospel Bethlehem is Joseph's home from the beginning.

With heavy strokes verse 4 underlines the Davidic origin of Joseph, the father of Jesus (see also 1:27). Whereas in 2:4 the town of David is specified as Bethlehem, it is left unspecified in verse 11 as if the shepherds should straightway know what is meant. This detail in verse 4 is very strange when we recall that in the Old Testament Jerusalem is the city of David— not Bethlehem. The puzzling nature of this reference invites us to peer behind the scene and spot an interpretation of Jesus' birth which issues from deep reflection upon God's revelation in the Old Testament. One key Old Testament text, which figures in this reflection, is 1 Samuel 17:12. It informs us that David stemmed from Bethlehem: "David was the son of an Ephrathite from Bethlehem of Judah whose name was Jesse." Since David hailed from Bethlehem, it could be called his city. But a more important text, also used by Matthew (see Mt 2:5–6), is a messianic prediction from the prophet Micah:

But you, Bethlehem Ephrathah,

the least of the clans of Judah,
out of you will be born for me
the one who is to rule over Israel. . . .
Yahweh is therefore going to abandon them
till the time when she who is to give birth gives
   birth. . . .

He will stand and feed his flock
with the power of Yahweh,
with the majesty of the name of his God. . . .
He himself will be peace. (Mi 5:1–4)

Jesus, the Messiah of David's line and longed for by
the prophet Micah, has been born in David's hometown, Bethlehem. The shepherding image in the latter
part of the quotation from Micah signals ahead Jesus'
role of feeding his people.

Jesus is explicitly called Mary's firstborn (2:7), so
that it will be patently clear that since he is the first-
born, he is heir to David's throne.

The Old Testament meditation on the meaning
of Jesus' birth continues in the latter half of verse 7:
"She wrapped him in swaddling clothes, and laid him
in a manger because there was no room for them at
the inn." The "swaddling clothes" allude to King Solomon's wisdom saying: "I was nurtured in swaddling
clothes, with every care. No king has known any other
beginning of existence" (Ws 7:4–5). Swaddling clothes
do not detract from Jesus' kingly status; even the great
King Solomon, David's son, wore the same garb at his
birth. The manger or feeding trough is vitally important
in our passage because it recurs in verses 12 and 16
as the sign for the shepherds. Jesus, who lies in a feeding trough, is food for the world. Furthermore, Luke's
source may also be drawing upon Isaiah 1:3: "The ox

knows its owner and the ass its master's crib. Israel
knows nothing, my people understands nothing." The
shepherds are representative of God's renewed people.
Unlike the people of Isaiah's time, they recognized their
master—in a crib, or manger. A final scriptural note:
Since Luke's tradition in this section interprets Jesus'
birth in Bethlehem so insightfully from the Old Testament, we should not press "there was no room for them
at the inn" too literally and scold the insensitive inn-
keepers who forced Jesus to be born in the cold out-
doors. There is some basis for thinking that a passage
like Jeremiah 14:8 is in view: "Yahweh, hope of Israel,
its savior in time of distress, why are you like a stranger
in this land, like a traveler who stays only for a night?"
Jesus has not come to his people to spend a night at
the local Holiday Inn. He takes up permanent residence
among them.

THE ANNUNCIATION OF JESUS' BIRTH AND ITS MEANING

2:8–14 The angelic message is the high point in the
interpretation of Jesus' birth. He is a joy for all the
people, the Savior, Christ the Lord; he, and not Caesar
Augustus, brings peace. At first blush, the lowly
shepherds, who work at David's profession, seem to be
the most unlikely candidates for such a revelation. A
Jewish tradition even goes so far as to maintain that
"the testimony of bandits, shepherds, and violent men,
and indeed all who are under suspicion when it comes
to money, is invalid." But as Luke will frequently point
out in his Gospel, Jesus has come for people of such
despised professions. And they are open to his revelation.

THE REACTIONS TO JESUS' REVELATION

2:15–20 The reactions to the revelation of Jesus are all positive and typical of the responses which Luke desires in his own readers. The shepherds react to what they have witnessed by sharing the message of the angels (2:17). All who hear the shepherds' message were led to further reflection on those events (2:18). Mary ponders what the shepherds have revealed about her son (2:19). The shepherds are the first spokespersons of the typical Lukan reaction of glorifying and praising God for Jesus (2:20). (See those passages where God is praised for a miracle which Jesus performs, e.g., 17:15; also see 23:47, where the centurion praises God for the revelation of God in Jesus' death on the cross.)

JESUS' CIRCUMCISION AND NAMING

2:21 By means of this verse Luke joins the tradition of 2:1–20 to the one he used earlier in 1:26–38, especially in 1:31. Unlike Matthew, Luke does not pause to interpret Jesus' name, which means Savior—"he is the one who is to save his people from their sins" (Mt 1:21).

STUDY QUESTIONS: Are today's equivalents of the lowly and despised shepherds as open as the shepherds to God's revelation in Jesus? Are the various reactions to the good news of Jesus mutually exclusive? When are we going to experience the peace which Jesus came to establish?

Luke 2:22–52
JESUS IS FOR ALL PEOPLE

22 And when the day came for them to be purified as laid down by the Law of Moses, they took him 23 up to Jerusalem to present him to the Lord—·observing what stands written in the Law of the Lord: Every first-born male must be consecrated 24 to the Lord—·also to offer in sacrifice, in accordance with what is said in the Law of the Lord, a 25 pair of turtledoves or two young pigeons. ·Now in Jerusalem there was a man named Simeon. He was an upright and devout man; he looked forward to Israel's comforting and the Holy Spirit 26 rested on him. ·It had been revealed to him by the Holy Spirit that he would not see death until he 27 had set eyes on the Christ of the Lord. ·Prompted by the Spirit he came to the Temple; and when the parents brought in the child Jesus to do for 28 him what the Law required, ·he took him into his arms and blessed God; and he said:

29 "Now, Master, you can let your servant go in peace,
   just as you promised;
30 because my eyes have seen the salvation
31 which you have prepared for all the nations to see,
32 a light to enlighten the pagans
   and the glory of your people Israel."

33 As the child's father and mother stood there wondering at the things that were being said about 34 him, ·Simeon blessed them and said to Mary his mother, "You see this child: he is destined for the fall and for the rising of many in Israel, des-35 tined to be a sign that is rejected—·and a sword

will pierce your own soul too—so that the secret thoughts of many may be laid bare."

36   There was a prophetess also, Anna the daughter of Phanuel, of the tribe of Asher. She was well on in years. Her days of girlhood over, she
37 had been married for seven years ·before becoming a widow. She was now eighty-four years old and never left the Temple, serving God night and
38 day with fasting and prayer. ·She came by just at that moment and began to praise God; and she spoke of the child to all who looked forward to the deliverance of Jerusalem.

39   When they had done everything the Law of the Lord required, they went back to Galilee, to their
40 own town of Nazareth. ·Meanwhile the child grew to maturity, and he was filled with wisdom; and God's favor was with him.

41   Every year his parents used to go to Jerusalem
42 for the feast of the Passover. ·When he was twelve years old, they went up for the feast as usual.
43 When they were on their way home after the feast, the boy Jesus stayed behind in Jerusalem
44 without his parents knowing it. ·They assumed he was with the caravan, and it was only after a day's journey that they went to look for him
45 among their relations and acquaintances. ·When they failed to find him they went back to Jerusalem looking for him everywhere.

46   Three days later, they found him in the Temple, sitting among the doctors, listening to them, and
47 asking them questions; ·and all those who heard him were astounded at his intelligence and his re-
48 plies. ·They were overcome when they saw him, and his mother said to him, "My child, why have you done this to us? See how worried your father
49 and I have been, looking for you." ·"Why were you looking for me?" he replied. "Did you not know that I must be busy with my Father's af-
50 fairs?" ·But they did not understand what he meant.

51   He then went down with them and came to

Nazareth and lived under their authority. His mother stored up all these things in her heart. ⁵² And Jesus increased in wisdom, in stature, and in favor with God and men.

✠

In this section Luke discontinues the parallelisms which have dominated his account so far and sounds the final bars of his theological overture. In his finale he repeats some earlier themes in a new key and introduces some powerful new motifs.

Jesus' parents, like John's (1:6), are described as faithful adherents of God's Law (2:22, 23, 27, 39, 41–42). As such, they are open to the revelation of the prophets Simeon and Anna, who give a dual witness to the meaning of Jesus to those who long for the deliverance of Jerusalem (2:38). Jesus, God's Son (1:35), is obedient to his Father's will (2:49). In this theological overture God's opening revelation occurred in the Temple; his revelation of his Son's meaning also occurs in the Temple on the lips of Simeon (2:29–35) and Jesus himself (2:49). When Jesus enters the Temple, he fulfills the messianic promise given by the prophet Malachi: "Look, I am going to send my messenger to prepare a way before me. And the Lord you are seeking will suddenly enter his Temple" (Ml 3:1). With Jesus in the Temple, the Temple itself is stripped of its meaning as a symbol of God's presence. In Jesus, God is really present among his people.

These final bars introduce two very important new motifs. The Jesus who is so graciously received by the lowly, Law-abiding, God-expecting Jewish people depicted in these chapters is also for the non-Jew. He is universal savior: "My eyes have seen the salvation which you have prepared for *all the nations* to see, a light to enlighten *the pagans* and the glory of your people Israel" (2:30–32). But as Savior and Messiah, Jesus' path will not be triumphalistic; he goes the way of suffering and martyrdom (2:34–35).

These verses form a rousing conclusion to Luke's theological overture and put the reader into the right set of mind to appreciate the story of Jesus which develops in the remainder of the Gospel.

The Adult John and Jesus;
Jesus' Galilean Ministry
Luke 3:1 to 9:50

Introduction to Luke 3:1 to 9:50
THE ADULT JOHN AND JESUS; JESUS' GALILEAN MINISTRY

With the melodies of his theological overture still ringing in our ears, Luke brings us to the first movement of his work. Whereas his "Infancy Narrative" (1:5 to 2:52) gave top billing to the childhood years of John the Baptist and Jesus, in 3:1 to 4:13 Luke headlines John and Jesus as adults and invites his readers to explore their significance in world and salvation history (3:1–6). In 3:7–20 Luke underlines how John's ministry prepares for Jesus'. By means of his descriptions of the baptism, genealogy, and temptations of Jesus (3:21 to 4:13), Luke gives greater insight into the significance of the Jesus whose public ministry in Galilee he will begin detailing in 4:14–30.

The theme of "God's fulfillment of his promises" dominates this first movement. In his inaugural sermon in Nazareth Jesus preaches that the prophecies of Isaiah will be fulfilled in his ministry: "The spirit of the Lord has been given to me, for he has anointed me. He has sent me to bring the good news to the poor, to proclaim liberty to captives and to the blind new sight, to set the downtrodden free, to proclaim the Lord's year of favor" (4:18–19). Luke enhances this theme by playing out the many ways in which a gracious God has smiled on people in Jesus' preaching and healing. As he befriends sinners and outcasts, eats with them, preaches good news to the poor, and cures the sick,

Jesus reveals the goodness of God. Since his message is not a flash in the pan, Jesus gathers the Twelve around him to continue his mission. But Jesus' message of God's graciousness is about as welcome as a prowler in one's home. Almost from the first hour of his ministry Jesus encounters misunderstanding and opposition (4:28–30). The grumbling of opposition crescendoes in chapter 9, where Jesus predicts that there's a cross in his future.

Underneath the music of this first movement one can detect some of Luke's contemporary concerns. A church which marches under the flag of Jesus must welcome sinners and outcasts if it's to be true to its colors. Opposition will be the church's traveling companion as it preaches and lives the good news that God is gracious. The cross that was in Jesus' future must light the church's way. Christians who are worth their salt will spend lifetimes playing the Jesus game: If you save your life, you lose it; but if you lose it for my sake, you'll gain it (9:24).

Luke 3:1–20
THE FEARLESS PREACHER
OF GENUINE CONVERSION

1 3 In the fifteenth year of Tiberius Caesar's reign, when Pontius Pilate was governor of Judaea, Herod tetrarch of Galilee, his brother Philip tetrarch of the lands of Ituraea and Trachonitis,
2 Lysanias tetrarch of Abilene, ·during the pontificate of Annas and Caiaphas, the word of God came to John son of Zechariah, in the wilderness.
3 He went through the whole Jordan district proclaiming a baptism of repentance for the forgive-
4 ness of sins, ·as it is written in the book of the sayings of the prophet Isaiah:

> A voice cries in the wilderness:
> Prepare a way for the Lord,
> make his paths straight.
5 Every valley will be filled in,
> every mountain and hill be laid low,
> winding ways will be straightened
> and rough roads made smooth.
6 And all mankind shall see the salvation of God.

7 He said, therefore, to the crowds who came to be baptized by him, "Brood of vipers, who warned you to fly from the retribution that is
8 coming? ·But if you are repentant, produce the appropriate fruits, and do not think of telling yourselves, 'We have Abraham for our father,' because, I tell you, God can raise children for
9 Abraham from these stones. ·Yes, even now the ax is laid to the roots of the trees, so that any tree which fails to produce good fruit will be cut down and thrown on the fire."
10 When all the people asked him, "What must

[11] we do, then?" ·he answered, "If anyone has two
tunics he must share with the man who has none,
and the one with something to eat must do the
[12] same." ·There were tax collectors too who came
for baptism, and these said to him, "Master, what
[13] must we do?" ·He said to them, "Exact no more
[14] than your rate." ·Some soldiers asked him in their
turn, "What about us? What must we do?" He
said to them, "No intimidation! No extortion! Be
content with your pay!"

[15]   A feeling of expectancy had grown among the
people, who were beginning to think that John
[16] might be the Christ, ·so John declared before
them all, "I baptize you with water, but someone
is coming, someone who is more powerful than I
am, and I am not fit to undo the strap of his sandals; he will baptize you with the Holy Spirit and
[17] fire. ·His winnowing fan is in his hand to clear his
threshing floor and to gather the wheat into his
barn; but the chaff he will burn in a fire that will
[18] never go out." ·As well as this, there were many
other things he said to exhort the people and to
announce the Good News to them.
[19]   But Herod the tetrarch, whom he criticized for
his relations with his brother's wife Herodias
and for all the other crimes Herod had commit-
[20] ted, ·added a further crime to all the rest by shut-
ting John up in prison.

✠

Careful reading through this section can nudge one's
memory into recalling some of the themes in Luke's
theological overture of chapter 1. "The word of God"
(3:2) comes to John the prophet (1:76). He gives his
people knowledge of God's salvation in Jesus (1:77),
a salvation which is for all people (3:6) and not restricted to those who can claim Abraham for their
father (3:8). Through his preaching John prepares "for
the Lord a people fit for him" (1:17).

The people who are fit for the Lord are those who go beyond lip service and actually produce the fruits of repentance. In 3:10–14, a passage which is found only in Luke's Gospel and which points ahead to one of his major themes, Luke gives examples of the fruits of repentance as care for and justice to one's fellow human beings. It is important to note who the people are who approach John for the baptism of repentance. It's the lowly and outcast people—and not the religious leaders—who are the people fit for the Lord (see 7:29–30 and the introduction to 19:45 to 23:56). The ability to trace one's lineage back to Abraham does not grant automatic entry into the ranks of God's people.

Despite his status as a fearless preacher and prophet of repentance, John is not the Christ. His preaching prepares the people for Jesus. Jesus, the future judge of all people (3:17), bestows salvation now on Luke's repentant readers through baptism in the Holy Spirit and the fire of Pentecost (3:16; see Ac 1:5 and 2:3–4).

STUDY QUESTION: What are the fruits of repentance asked of us today as a sign that our baptism means something to us?

Luke 3:21–38
JESUS, THOROUGHLY HUMAN
AND GOD'S SON

21 Now when all the people had been baptized and while Jesus after his own baptism was at prayer,
22 heaven opened ·and the Holy Spirit descended on him in bodily shape, like a dove. And a voice came from heaven, "You are my Son, the Beloved; my favor rests on you."
23 When he started to teach, Jesus was about thirty
24 years old, being the son, ·as it was thought, of Joseph son of Heli, son of Matthat, son of Levi,
25 son of Melchi, son of Jannai, son of Joseph, ·son of Mattathias, son of Amos, son of Nahum, son
26 of Esli, son of Naggai, ·son of Maath, son of Mattathias, son of Semein, son of Josech, son of Joda,
27 son of Joanan, son of Rhesa, son of Zerubbabel,
28 son of Shealtiel, son of Neri, ·son of Melchi, son of Addi, son of Cosam, son of Elmadam, son
29 of Er, ·son of Joshua, son of Eliezer, son
30 of Jorim, son of Matthat, son of Levi, ·son of Symeon, son of Judah, son of Joseph, son of
31 Jonam, son of Eliakim, ·son of Melea, son of Menna, son of Mattatha, son of Nathan, son of
32 David, ·son of Jesse, son of Obed, son of Boaz,
33 son of Sala, son of Nahshon, ·son of Amminadab, son of Admin, son of Arni, son of Hezron, son of
34 Perez, son of Judah, ·son of Jacob, son of Isaac,
35 son of Abraham, son of Terah, son of Nahor, ·son of Serug, son of Reu, son of Peleg, son of Eber,
36 son of Shelah, ·son of Cainan, son of Arphaxad,
37 son of Shem, son of Noah, son of Lamech, ·son of Methuselah, son of Enoch, son of Jared, son
38 of Mahalaleel, son of Cainan, ·son of Enos, son of Seth, son of Adam, son of God.

✠

Luke's accounts of Jesus' baptism and genealogy are packed with clues as to Jesus' significance. But we will have to marshall our best weather-eye alertness if we are not to miss these clues.

The account of Jesus' baptism (3:21–22) has two main clues: the Holy Spirit, and the declaration from heaven. While at prayer (On prayer in Luke, see the commentary on 11:1–13), Jesus receives the Holy Spirit. As we noted in the commentary on 1:5–38, there is a tension between the account of Jesus' baptism and the account of his virginal conception in 1:35: "The Holy Spirit will come upon you." When we look at these accounts as two sides of the same Lukan coin, we see that this tension is not destructive but creative. Viewed in conjunction with 1:35, 3:22 does not teach that the completely human Jesus was first adopted by the Holy Spirit to be God's Son at his baptism. What Jesus had been since his conception is now dramatized at the baptism of the adult Jesus. For its part, the baptism account underlines the thoroughly human side of Jesus; Jesus does not sport some sort of nonhuman body because he was virginally conceived. The revelation from heaven illumines Jesus' status from another angle. Endowed with the power of God's Spirit, Jesus must carry out his unique commission as God's Son. Like Israel of old, Jesus is God's Son, the beginning of God's new people, and must gather folk into that people.

Luke's genealogy of Jesus is high theology and should not be read like a list of names in a telephone directory. This clue-studded passage traces Jesus' lineage through the Old Testament back to David and

Abraham. Thus, Jesus stands in the line of what God
has done for his people. Jesus' lineage is also traced
back to Adam, to show that he has significance not only
for the Jewish people but for all peoples. Just as the
first Adam was a unique creation of God, so too does
the second Adam, Jesus, have a unique origin in God.

STUDY QUESTION: To what extent do the clues of this
section contribute to our under-
standing of Luke's portrait of Jesus?

Luke 4:1–13
JESUS, SON OF GOD,
CONQUERS THE RULER OF THIS WORLD

¹ 4 Filled with the Holy Spirit, Jesus left the Jordan and was led by the Spirit through the wil-
² derness, ·being tempted there by the devil for forty days. During that time he ate nothing and at the
³ end he was hungry. ·Then the devil said to him, "If you are the Son of God, tell this stone to turn
⁴ into a loaf." ·But Jesus replied, "Scripture says: Man does not live on bread alone."

⁵ Then leading him to a height, the devil showed him in a moment of time all the kingdoms of the
⁶ world ·and said to him, "I will give you all this power and the glory of these kingdoms, for it has been committed to me and I give it to anyone I
⁷ choose. ·Worship me, then, and it shall all be
⁸ yours." ·But Jesus answered him, "Scripture says:

You must worship the Lord your God,
and serve him alone."

⁹ Then he led him to Jerusalem and made him stand on the parapet of the Temple. "If you are the Son of God," he said to him, "throw your-
¹⁰ self down from here, ·for scripture says:

He will put his angels in charge of you
to guard you,

and again:

¹¹ They will hold you up on their hands
in case you hurt your foot against a stone."

¹² But Jesus answered him, "It has been said:

You must not put the Lord your God to the
test."

¹⁸ Having exhausted all these ways of tempting him,
the devil left him, to return at the appointed time.

☩

This section resembles an exquisitely beautiful diamond and the setting which a master craftsman can
create for it. By itself the diamond enthralls us with
its beauty. Give that same diamond to a master jeweler,
and he will fashion a setting for it which will summon
our attention to hitherto unseen facets of its beauty.

Jesus' three responses to the devil's testing are from
Deuteronomy (Dt 8:3, 6:13, 6:16) and are the diamond of this section. Deuteronomy 8:2 provides the
background for this testing: "Remember how Yahweh
your God led you for forty years in the wilderness, to
humble you, to test you and know your inmost heart—
whether you would keep his commandments or not."
Jesus, who embodies the new Israel of God's people,
is not like the Israel of old, which did not endure its
testing in the wilderness.

Luke has placed this diamond into a multiply rich
setting and thereby enhanced its meaning. When the
devil tests Jesus, "If you are the Son of God"
(4:3, 9), Luke refers his readers back to Jesus' baptism, where God had declared, "You are my Son"
(3:22). Jesus, God's Son, is faithful to his Father and
does not fall during his testing as Israel, God's Son, had
done. Luke's insertion of the genealogy between Jesus'
baptism and his testing reveals another feature of his
rich setting. The genealogy ends with "Adam, son of
God" (3:38). Unlike the first Adam, Jesus, Son of
God, emerges victorious from his testing.

The most brilliant features of Luke's setting sparkle in the modifications he has made in the account of Jesus' testing, an account which he has in common with Matthew. Luke underscores the fact that the testing of Jesus is solely the devil's doing (4:1–2). Compare Matthew 4:1, where the Spirit is also involved in Jesus' testing. In verse 6 Luke emphasizes that the devil is lord of the world. Contrast Matthew's more prosaic version (Mt 4:8). Luke uses these changes to arrange the diamond of Jesus, the new Israel, in a cosmic setting. Jesus' significance lies in his conquest of the ruler of this world.

Master jeweler that he is, Luke adds one final touch to the setting he has fashioned for his diamond. For Luke, Jesus' testing in Jerusalem is the final and climactic testing. It is in Jerusalem that the devil will return "at the appointed time" (4:13; see 22:3, 53). As Jesus is on the brink of his public ministry, Luke directs our attention to Jerusalem, where God's promises will be ultimately fulfilled.

STUDY QUESTION: Is the victorious Jesus presented in this section a model for Christians when they are tested?

JESUS' VISION OF HIS MINISTRY

¹⁴ Jesus, with the power of the Spirit in him, returned to Galilee; and his reputation spread
¹⁵ throughout the countryside. ·He taught in their synagogues and everyone praised him.

¹⁶ He came to Nazara, where he had been brought up, and went into the synagogue on the sabbath
¹⁷ day as he usually did. He stood up to read, ·and they handed him the scroll of the prophet Isaiah. Unrolling the scroll he found the place where it is written:

¹⁸ The spirit of the Lord has been given to me,
   for he has anointed me.
   He has sent me to bring the good news to the
      poor,
   to proclaim liberty to captives
   and to the blind new sight,
   to set the downtrodden free,
¹⁹ to proclaim the Lord's year of favor.

²⁰ He then rolled up the scroll, gave it back to the assistant and sat down. And all eyes in the syna-
²¹ gogue were fixed on him. ·Then he began to speak to them, "This text is being fulfilled today even
²² as you listen." ·And he won the approval of all, and they were astonished by the gracious words that came from his lips.

²³ They said, "This is Joseph's son, surely?" ·But he replied, "No doubt you will quote me the say-ing, 'Physician, heal yourself,' and tell me, 'We have heard all that happened in Capernaum, do
²⁴ the same here in your own countryside.'" ·And

he went on, "I tell you solemnly, no prophet is ever accepted in his own country.

25 "There were many widows in Israel, I can assure you, in Elijah's day, when heaven remained shut for three years and six months and a great
26 famine raged throughout the land, ·but Elijah was not sent to any of these: he was sent to a widow
27 at Zarephath, a Sidonian town. ·And in the prophet Elisha's time there were many lepers in Israel, but none of these was cured, except the Syrian, Naaman."

28 When they heard this everyone in the syna-
29 gogue was enraged. ·They sprang to their feet and hustled him out of the town; and they took him up to the brow of the hill their town was built
30 on, intending to throw him down the cliff, ·but he slipped through the crowd and walked away.

✠

Now that he has briefed his readers about the primal significance of Jesus (1:5 to 4:13), Luke turns their attention to Jesus' Galilean ministry (4:14 to 9:50).

Jesus' inaugural sermon in his hometown synagogue (4:16–21) might be likened to a U.S. President's inauguration speech. In that speech the President defines his goals and conveys a vision of what he plans to accomplish during the next four years. Jesus preaches that God's prophecies in Isaiah 61:1–2 and 58:6 are being fulfilled in his ministry; these prophecies define his goals. Isaiah 58:6–7 points to the social dimension of Jesus' ministry: "Is not this the sort of fast that pleases me—to break unjust fetters and undo the thongs of the yoke, to let the oppressed go free, and break every yoke, to share your bread with the hungry, and shelter the homeless poor?" Although Jesus' ministry surely has a social dimension, it cannot be equated with mere social action. The Greek word translated by "liberty" and "free" in 4:18 is also used by Luke for *forgiveness* of sins (see, for example, 1:77, 24:47). The liberty and freedom which Jesus brings is liberation from the oppression of sin. Luke goes out of his way in the chapters which follow to show how Jesus' ministry flowed from the vision projected in his inaugural sermon. See the summary passages 4:40–41, 5:15, 6:17–19, and especially 7:20–22.

Like a President's inauguration address, Jesus' inaugural sermon meets with reaction (4:22–30). Or to change the image, it's like a new President returning to his own hometown and telling his people that they are not going to get any preferential treatment just because he hails from their town. The four years of favor are for *all* the nation's poor, captive, blind, and downtrodden. As the examples of Elijah and Elisha show (4:25–27), God's mercy and favor extend beyond the borders of the hometown gang, the chosen people. God's fulfillment of his promises in Jesus' ministry does not spell immediate bliss for the hometown folk and consummate catastrophe for outsiders. As we have noted in Mary's Magnificat (1:46–55), reversal of status is the bedfellow of God's fulfillment of his promises. The haves become the have-nots. We also catch a glimmer of a theme which will be developed in Acts: Whereas the majority of God's people refuse to believe the Christian message, the non-Jews receive it gladly. We also spy the cross of Jesus looming on the horizon. His rejection at Nazareth is the first of many such.

STUDY QUESTION: Must all ministry which prides itself on being Christian espouse Christ's vision of his ministry found in Luke 4:16–21?

JESUS IS THE WINDOW TO GOD

³¹ He went down to Capernaum, a town in Gali-
³² lee, and taught them on the sabbath. ·And his
teaching made a deep impression on them be-
cause he spoke with authority.

³³ In the synagogue there was a man who was pos-
sessed by the spirit of an unclean devil, and it
³⁴ shouted at the top of its voice, ·"Ha! What do
you want with us, Jesus of Nazareth? Have you
come to destroy us? I know who you are: the
³⁵ Holy One of God." ·But Jesus said sharply, "Be
quiet! Come out of him!" And the devil, throwing
the man down in front of everyone, went out of
³⁶ him without hurting him at all. ·Astonishment
seized them and they were all saying to one another, "What teaching! He gives orders to unclean spirits with authority and power and they
³⁷ come out." ·And reports of him went all through
the surrounding countryside.

³⁸ Leaving the synagogue he went to Simon's
house. Now Simon's mother-in-law was suffering
from a high fever and they asked him to do some-
³⁹ thing for her. ·Leaning over her he rebuked the
fever and it left her. And she immediately got up
and began to wait on them.

⁴⁰ At sunset all those who had friends suffering
from diseases of one kind or another brought
them to him, and laying his hands on each he
⁴¹ cured them. ·Devils too came out of many people,
howling, "You are the Son of God." But he re-
buked them and would not allow them to speak
because they knew that he was the Christ.

⁴² When daylight came he left the house and made
his way to a lonely place. The crowds went to

look for him, and when they had caught up with
⁴³ him they wanted to prevent him leaving them, ·but
he answered, "I must proclaim the Good News
of the kingdom of God to the other towns too,
⁴⁴ because that is what I was sent to do." ·And he
continued his preaching in the synagogues of
Judaea.

✠

The key to understanding this section is the phrase,
"the kingdom of God" (4:43). This phrase is like the
refrain in Martin Luther King, Jr.'s "I Have a Dream"
speech. The refrain "I have a dream" sweeps all that
goes before and after it into its interpretive train and
becomes a meditative rallying point. Throughout his
work Luke repeats the refrain "the kingdom of God,"
to lure his readers away from fixating on individual sayings and deeds of Jesus, so that they can meditate on
the significance of the Jesus who pronounces these individual sayings and performs these individual deeds.
In repeating this refrain, Luke draws upon the Old
Testament image of God's kingdom, an image which
points to the rule which God exercises and will exercise
to establish peace, health, justice, and forgiveness in
this world. Caught between foreign domination and the
devil's oppressive tactics of sickness and disease, the
people of Jesus' time longed for a renewed expression
of God's rule on their behalf. What is paramount for
Luke is that God's kingdom is no longer just an expectation; God's rule is present in the deeds and teaching
of Jesus (see 7:22 and 17:21).

In the section at hand, "to proclaim the Good News
of the kingdom of God" (4:43) casts an interpretive
net over the two miracles which Jesus works by a mere
word (4:31–39). Besides illustrating the authority and

effectiveness of Jesus' teaching (4:32, 36), these deeds
single out Jesus as the one who brings about God's rule
by restoring health to both men (4:33–37) and women
(4:38–39). In Jesus' ministry God's rule makes inroads
against the devil which holds men and women captive
(see 4:18 and 13:16). As Son of God (4:41), Jesus
continues the attack on the devil which began in the
wilderness (4:1–13). In Jesus, God shows what he and
his rule are like.

STUDY QUESTION: Is the church involved in making
                God's rule present today?

Luke 5:1–11
SIMON PETER, JESUS' APOSTLE,
BY THE GRACE OF GOD

¹ 5 Now he was standing one day by the Lake of Gennesaret, with the crowd pressing around ² him listening to the word of God, ·when he caught sight of two boats close to the bank. The fishermen had gone out of them and were washing their ³ nets. ·He got into one of the boats—it was Simon's —and asked him to put out a little from the shore. Then he sat down and taught the crowds from the boat.

⁴ When he had finished speaking he said to Simon, "Put out into deep water and pay out your ⁵ nets for a catch." ·"Master," Simon replied, "we worked hard all night long and caught nothing, ⁶ but if you say so, I will pay out the nets." ·And when they had done this they netted such a huge ⁷ number of fish that their nets began to tear, ·so they signaled to their companions in the other boat to come and help them; when these came, they filled the two boats to sinking point.

⁸ When Simon Peter saw this he fell at the knees of Jesus saying, "Leave me, Lord; I am a sinful ⁹ man." ·For he and all his companions were com- ¹⁰ pletely overcome by the catch they had made; ·so also were James and John, sons of Zebedee, who were Simon's partners. But Jesus said to Simon, "Do not be afraid; from now on it is men you ¹¹ will catch." ·Then, bringing their boats back to land, they left everything and followed him.

✠

Luke has drawn much of his material for Jesus' Galilean ministry (4:14 to 9:50) from his source, the Gospel of Mark. A comparison of Luke's account of Simon's call with Mark's will uncover the message of this section. Mark writes:

> As he was walking along the Sea of Galilee he saw Simon and his brother Andrew casting a net in the lake—for they were fishermen. And Jesus said to them, "Follow me and I will make you into fishers of men." And at once they left their nets and followed him. (Mk 1:16–18)

It is obvious that the huge catch of fish (5:4–7) and Simon's reaction to it (5:8–11) lengthen Luke's version. A simile will help us explore the meaning of Luke's fuller account. The miracle of the catch of fish is not introduced for its own sake. It's like an anecdote which illustrates a point. Recall the anecdote frequently told about Pope John XXIII. When asked how many people worked in the Vatican, the Pope replied, "About half of them." The anecdote illustrates the warm sense of humor which John XXIII possessed.

The story of the miraculous catch of fish leads into Simon's reaction. In the same way that Jesus' command, "Pay out your nets" (5:4), is effective in the catch of fish, so Jesus' "From now on it is men you will catch" (5:10) will be effective in Simon's ministry. Just as the spectacular catch of fish is Jesus' pure gift to Simon, so too is Jesus' commissioning of Simon to be an apostle pure gift. Jesus befriends the sinful Simon (5:8) and enlists him in his corps of kingdom workers.

One final point. By his addition of "left *everything*" (5:11), Luke adds another building block to his theme of poor and rich (see the commentary on Lk 18:15–

30). The experience of Jesus' powerful words and deeds in one's life can become a summons to leave all and accept the call to apostolic mission.

STUDY QUESTION: Are we as open as Simon to Jesus' startling message that God is very fond of sinners?

Luke 5:12 to 6:11
JESUS EFFECTS GOD'S KINGDOM
WHILE OPPOSITION MOUNTS

12   Now Jesus was in one of the towns when a man appeared, covered with leprosy. Seeing Jesus he fell on his face and implored him. "Sir," he said,
13   "if you want to, you can cure me." ·Jesus stretched out his hand, touched him and said, "Of course I want to! Be cured!" And the leprosy left him at
14   once. ·He ordered him to tell no one, "But go and show yourself to the priest and make the offering for your healing as Moses prescribed it, as evidence for them."

15   His reputation continued to grow, and large crowds would gather to hear him and to have their
16   sickness cured, ·but he would always go off to some place where he could be alone and pray.

17   Now he was teaching one day, and among the audience there were Pharisees and doctors of the Law who had come from every village in Galilee, from Judaea and from Jerusalem. And the Power of the Lord was behind his works of healing.
18   Then some men appeared, carrying on a bed a paralyzed man whom they were trying to bring
19   in and lay down in front of him. ·But as the crowd made it impossible to find a way of getting him in, they went up on to the flat roof and lowered him and his stretcher down through the tiles into the middle of the gathering, in front of Jesus.
20   Seeing their faith he said, "My friend, your sins
21   are forgiven you." ·The scribes and the Pharisees began to think this over. "Who is this man talking blasphemy? Who can forgive sins but God
22   alone?" ·But Jesus, aware of their thoughts, made them this reply, "What are these thoughts you

²³ have in your hearts? ·Which of these is easier: to
say, 'Your sins are forgiven you' or to say, 'Get
²⁴ up and walk?' ·But to prove to you that the Son
of Man has authority on earth to forgive sins,"
—he said to the paralyzed man—"I order you:
get up, and pick up your stretcher and go home."
²⁵ And immediately before their very eyes he got
up, picked up what he had been lying on and
went home praising God.

²⁶   They were all astounded and praised God, and
were filled with awe, saying, "We have seen
strange things today."

²⁷   When he went out after this, he noticed a tax
collector, Levi by name, sitting by the customs
²⁸ house, and said to him, "Follow me." ·And leaving everything he got up and followed him.

²⁹   In his honor Levi held a great reception in his
house, and with them at table was a large gather-
³⁰ ing of tax collectors and others. ·The Pharisees
and their scribes complained to his disciples and
said, "Why do you eat and drink with tax col-
³¹ lectors and sinners?" ·Jesus said to them in reply,
"It is not those who are well who need the doctor,
³² but the sick. ·I have not come to call the virtuous,
but sinners to repentance."

³³   They then said to him, "John's disciples are always fasting and saying prayers, and the disciples
of the Pharisees too, but yours go on eating
³⁴ and drinking." ·Jesus replied, "Surely you cannot
make the bridegroom's attendants fast while the
³⁵ bridegroom is still with them? ·But the time will
come, the time for the bridegroom to be taken
away from them; that will be the time when they
will fast."

³⁶   He also told them this parable, "No one tears
a piece from a new cloak to put it on an old
cloak; if he does, not only will he have torn the
new one, but the piece taken from the new will
not match the old.

³⁷   "And nobody puts new wine into old skins; if
he does, the new wine will burst the skins and

38 then run out, and the skins will be lost. ·No; new
39 wine must be put into fresh skins. ·And nobody
who has been drinking old wine wants new. 'The
old is good,' he says."

1   6 Now one sabbath he happened to be taking a
    walk through the cornfields, and his disciples
were picking ears of corn, rubbing them in their
2 hands and eating them. ·Some of the Pharisees
said, "Why are you doing something that is for-
3 bidden on the sabbath day?" ·Jesus answered
them, "So you have not read what David did
4 when he and his followers were hungry—·how he
went into the house of God, took the loaves of
offering and ate them and gave them to his followers, loaves which only the priests are allowed
5 to eat?" ·And he said to them, "The Son of Man
is master of the sabbath."

6   Now on another sabbath he went into the synagogue and began to teach, and a man was there
7 whose right hand was withered. ·The scribes and
the Pharisees were watching him to see if he
would cure a man on the sabbath, hoping to find
8 something to use against him. ·But he knew their
thoughts; and he said to the man with the withered hand, "Stand up! Come out into the middle."
9 And he came out and stood there. ·Then Jesus
said to them, "I put it to you: is it against the
law on the sabbath to do good, or to do evil; to
10 save life, or to destroy it?" ·Then he looked
around at them all and said to the man, "Stretch
out your hand." He did so, and his hand was bet-
11 ter. ·But they were furious, and began to discuss
the best way of dealing with Jesus.

☩

In this section Luke follows Mark's sequence most
closely (Mk 1:40 to 3:6). In doing so, he crisscrosses
many themes and operates on a number of levels.

On one level Luke uses this material to spell out in

more detail how Jesus brings about God's kingdom. In fulfillment of God's promises (see 4:18 and 7:22), Jesus cleanses a leper and restores him to community life and worship (5:12–16). When Jesus heals a paralytic, he scores another knockdown on the devil which holds people captive in the bonds of sickness. In Jesus, God's rule works for the forgiveness of sins (5:17–26). Jesus calls the despised toll collector Levi to follow him and gives most visible expression to God's rule of mercy by supping with him. As he embraces sinners with the arms of full acceptance by eating with them, Jesus images God's kingdom as a banquet (5:27–32; see Is 25:6–12). For his part Levi evidences his acceptance of Jesus' forgiveness by his repentance (5:32) in leaving everything (5:28). Jesus' mission is so God-studded that he has authority over the divine ordinance of the sabbath (6:1–5). His mission of doing good and saving life is more important than mere sabbath observance (6:6–11).

On another level Luke operates with the theme of opposition. In effecting God's rule, Jesus brings the unexpected and is harassed by the Pharisees and scribes who are so sure that their mature way of viewing God and his activity is correct that they are not able to bring the new way of Jesus into focus (5:39). Jesus' claim to forgive sins beckons them to see Jesus with new eyes, but they continue to use their old categories and cry out, "Blasphemy" (5:21). How can Jesus be from God and defile himself by eating with sinners (5:30)? Why doesn't Jesus observe our sabbath regulations (6:2, 7, 11)? The note of opposition, sounded in 4:16–30, builds up volume in this section and reaches a high point in 6:11.

On still another level Luke's message is addressed to Theophilus and his kin (1:1–4), who need assurances

for their religious faith and practices amidst opposition
from the "Pharisees" of their day. Theophilus and company are in Luke's sights in 5:30 and 33 and 6:2 where
he highlights the disciples and leaves Jesus in the background. Luke's Christians have been cleansed and forgiven, and must share table fellowship with sinners
despite the popular vote of no confidence (5:30). They
fast, but not frequently (5:33). Following the Lord of
the sabbath, they must allow the norm of love of neighbor to free them from legalistic tendencies (6:2).

Luke's church is encouraged to continue Jesus' mission, to build its religious faith and practices on the
basis of his words and deeds, and to withstand the
winds of opposition blowing in its day.

STUDY QUESTION: It's easy for us adept second-
guessers to reprimand the stodgy
Pharisees of Jesus' day for failing to
follow Jesus. On a scale of one to
ten, do we score higher than they in
our befriending of outcasts and sinners?

Luke 6:12–16
THE REBUILDERS OF GOD'S PEOPLE

12 Now it was about this time that he went out into the hills to pray; and he spent the whole
13 night in prayer to God. ·When day came he summoned his disciples and picked out twelve of
14 them; he called them "apostles": ·Simon whom he called Peter, and his brother Andrew; James,
15 John, Philip, Bartholomew, ·Matthew, Thomas, James son of Alphaeus, Simon called the Zealot,
16 Judas son of James, and Judas Iscariot who became a traitor.

✠

Prayer. The Twelve. Apostles. To dig behind the meaning of these key words, let's imagine ourselves being challenged by the questions little children pop to their parents: "What's that mean?" "Why?" Why did Jesus pray? Why did he choose just twelve? What's an apostle?

As he does so often in his Gospel, Luke spotlights Jesus at prayer (6:12; see the commentary on Lk 11:1–13). The selection of the Twelve is not only Jesus' decision, but also God's will revealed in prayer.

Why just twelve? Wouldn't a hundred do the job more effectively? We can open a door on the significance of the number twelve by recalling that God's people Israel was built upon twelve tribes. Although unity under the twelve tribes dissolved, the twelve-tribe federation continued to serve as a model for God's rebuilding of his people. Just as the Old Testament Israel was built upon the twelve tribes and their leaders, so the Israel which Jesus constitutes is built upon twelve leaders. The Twelve point beyond themselves to what God is doing through Jesus. He is rebuilding his people, Israel.

An apostle—the word means "one sent"—represents the one who sends him much as a high-ranking dignitary sent by the President of the United States to a peace conference represents him and is invested with much of his authority. The apostles represent Jesus, the bringer of God's kingdom. In Luke the apostles also give public testimony to Jesus' significance by witnessing to his earthly life and resurrection. In Peter's guidelines on how to replace Judas and thus fill up the number of twelve apostles, this notion of witness shines through clearly: "We must therefore choose someone who has been with us the whole time that the Lord Jesus was traveling around with us . . . he can act with us as a *witness* to his resurrection" (Acts 1:21–22). Luke has combined the notion of the Twelve with apostle. The task of the twelve apostles is to represent and witness to Jesus as God's promised Messiah and to rebuild God's people on the foundation of that Jesus.

STUDY QUESTION: We frequently hear that the church must be apostolic. What does that really mean?

Luke 6:17–26
SETTING THE WORLD'S STANDARDS
ON THEIR HEAD

¹⁷ He then came down with them and stopped at a piece of level ground where there was a large gathering of his disciples with a great crowd of people from all parts of Judaea and from Jerusalem and from the coastal region of Tyre and ¹⁸ Sidon ·who had come to hear him and to be cured of their diseases. People tormented by unclean ¹⁹ spirits were also cured, ·and everyone in the crowd was trying to touch him because power came out of him that cured them all.

²⁰ Then fixing his eyes on his disciples he said:

"How happy are you who are poor: yours is the kingdom of God.
²¹ Happy you who are hungry now: you shall be satisfied.
Happy you who weep now: you shall laugh.

²² "Happy are you when people hate you, drive you out, abuse you, denounce your name as criminal, on account of the Son of Man. ·Rejoice when ²³ that day comes and dance for joy, then your reward will be great in heaven. This was the way their ancestors treated the prophets.

²⁴ "But alas for you who are rich: you are having your consolation now.
²⁵ Alas for you who have your fill now: you shall go hungry.
Alas for you who laugh now: you shall mourn and weep.

²⁶ "Alas for you when the world speaks well of

you! This was the way their ancestors treated the
false prophets.

✠

This section begins Luke's Sermon on the Plain
(6:17–49), which contains the blueprints for the rebuilding of God's people, Israel.

In verse 20 Luke catches our attention with the refrain, "kingdom of God," and signals us to meditate
once more on Jesus' kingdom ministry. The kingdom
of God images the mercy which the king extended to
the oppressed, neglected, and poor. This aspect of the
kingdom image is front and center stage in this section.

Let's use an example to think ourselves into this aspect of God's rule which Jesus brings. Suppose a poll-
ster phoned you and asked what indicators would best
describe happiness for you: "Would you equate happiness with being poor, hungry, sorrowful, and being
despised by everyone? Or would you equate happiness
with abundant money, a well-set table, joy, and being
held in high regard by everyone?" No doubt you would
choose the last set of indicators. Yet Jesus' beatitudes
and woes challenge us to rethink our choice as they turn
the world's standards on their head. The kingdom
which Jesus brings is a frontal attack on the evil by
which people are made economically poor and oppressed. The oppressed and deprived are favored by
God, not because they happen to be poor and have no
need to repent, but because God the king is merciful.
The rich and well-fed also need repentance and must
not allow the goods and standards of this world to turn
their hands against the poor and God's rule in Jesus.

Luke transmits Jesus' kingdom preaching to his own
community. The beatitudes and woes, which were first

addressed to the general public of Jesus' day, are now
addressed to the "disciples" of Luke's day (6:20). All
have already experienced the rule of Jesus the Lord in
their own lives. But God's kingdom of justice and
mercy has not come in its fullness. Some members of
Luke's community are still poor, and are persecuted because of their allegiance to Jesus. These are consoled
that, despite signs to the contrary, God's rule will be
triumphant in the end. The rich members of Luke's
community are warned that wealth is not the be-all and
end-all of life. They should not compromise their faith
in Jesus to avoid persecution and confiscation of their
property. They should befriend their poor and persecuted fellow Christians.

STUDY QUESTION: Is there anything we can do today
                to promote God's kingdom of mercy
                and justice?

Luke 6:27–35
THE LOVE ETHIC OF THE KINGDOM

27 "But I say this to you who are listening: Love your enemies, do good to those who hate you,
28 bless those who curse you, pray for those who
29 treat you badly. ·To the man who slaps you on one cheek, present the other cheek too; to the man who takes your cloak from you, do not re-
30 fuse your tunic. ·Give to everyone who asks you, and do not ask for your property back from the
31 man who robs you. ·Treat others as you would
32 like them to treat you. ·If you love those who love you, what thanks can you expect? Even sinners
33 love those who love them. ·And if you do good to those who do good to you, what thanks can you
34 expect? For even sinners do that much. ·And if you lend to those from whom you hope to re- ceive, what thanks can you expect? Even sinners
35 lend to sinners to get back the same amount. ·In- stead, love your enemies and do good, and lend without any hope of return. You will have a great reward, and you will be sons of the Most High, for he himself is kind to the ungrateful and the wicked.

✠

The love ethic of the kingdom is the heart of this section. Jesus preaches the almost-too-good-to-be-true news that the motive force behind God's rule is love. He's not mean and tyrannical. He's kind (6:35); he's a compassionate father (6:36). Those who accept Jesus' message that God is merciful must reflect that

same mercy in their own lives. They must love their
enemies (6:27, 35). For them the Golden Rule is life's
norm: "Treat others as you would like them to treat
you" (6:31).

Realizing that Jesus' love ethic is general, Luke applies it to two specific concerns within his community:
the persecuted, and the possessors. In verses 27–31 the
plight of the persecuted is portrayed in graphic detail:
They are hated, cursed, maltreated, slapped around,
and robbed. Although they are treated like the village
idiot, these Christians are to treat their persecutors as
they themselves would like to be treated (6:31). In
verses 32–35 Luke applies the love ethic to the possessors within his community. They must cease and desist
from the tit-for-tat ethic which is part and parcel of the
cultural air they breathe, an ethic which limits their
charity to those who have the wherewithal to return
the favor. Such self-serving charity must give way to
Jesus' love ethic (see the commentary on 14:12–14).

Before we decry Jesus' love ethic as an invitation to
joust with a windmill, let's remember that this ethic is
addressed to disciples (6:20), to children of the Most
High (6:35), to those who have been showered with
the transforming love of God's rule and enabled to test
the waters of the seemingly impossible.

STUDY QUESTION: Does Luke's application of Jesus'
                love ethic provide us with guidelines
                on how we might apply that ethic
                today?

Luke 6:36–49
THE PROOF OF DISCIPLESHIP
IS IN THE DOING

36 "Be compassionate as your Father is compas-
37 sionate. ·Do not judge, and you will not be judged
yourselves; do not condemn, and you will not be
condemned yourselves: grant pardon, and you
38 will be pardoned. ·Give, and there will be gifts for
you: a full measure, pressed down, shaken together, and running over, will be poured into your
lap; because the amount you measure out is the
amount you will be given back."

39 He also told a parable to them, "Can one blind
man guide another? Surely both will fall into a
40 pit? ·The disciple is not superior to his teacher;
the fully trained disciple will always be like his
41 teacher. ·Why do you observe the splinter in your
brother's eye and never notice the plank in your
42 own? ·How can you say to your brother, 'Brother,
let me take out the splinter that is in your eye,'
when you cannot see the plank in your own?
Hypocrite! Take the plank out of your own eye
first, and then you will see clearly enough to take
out the splinter that is in your brother's eye.

43 "There is no sound tree that produces rotten
fruit, nor again a rotten tree that produces sound
44 fruit. ·For every tree can be told by its own fruit:
people do not pick figs from thorns, nor gather
45 grapes from brambles. ·A good man draws what
is good from the store of goodness in his heart;
a bad man draws what is bad from the store of
badness. For a man's words flow out of what fills
his heart.

46 "Why do you call me, 'Lord, Lord' and not do
what I say?

47   "Everyone who comes to me and listens to my
     words and acts on them—I will show you what
48   he is like. ·He is like the man who when he built
     his house dug, and dug deep, and laid the founda-
     tions on rock; when the river was in flood it bore
     down on that house but could not shake it, it was
49   so well built. ·But the one who listens and does
     nothing is like the man who built his house on
     soil, with no foundations: as soon as the river
     bore down on it, it collapsed; and what a ruin that
     house became!"

✠

Luke concludes Jesus' Sermon on the Plain with
three messages. In 6:36–38 he rounds off the meaning
of the love ethic of the kingdom. Disciples must share
with one another the mercy they have received from
God. To the extent that they show mercy, they will receive mercy from God.

In 6:39–45 church leaders, the "fully trained disciples" (6:40), are addressed. They must not parade
around telling everyone else to look into the mirror of
the love ethic. While busily telling others that they have
a slight bit of egg on their cheek, they fail to glance
into the mirror themselves and see traces of breakfast
all over their face and a pimple ripening on the tip of
their nose. Christians' actions will show whether the
love ethic is the center of their lives (6:43–45).

Jesus' love ethic is not to be mouthed, but done
(6:46–49). Since Jesus proclaims and brings about
God's rule, he can promise that those who lay a foundation on his teaching will escape the catastrophe of the
flood. "Lord, Lord" is to be informed with an obedi-
ence to Jesus which stems from love, a love whose
flame will not die out when persecution rages, when the
rich and church leaders give scandal, and when false

teachers proclaim that the confession "Lord, Lord" speaks louder than actions done in one's despicable body.

STUDY QUESTION: The Sermon on the Plain can be described as a pattern for Christian life. Should this pattern be followed rigidly or creatively?

¹ 7 When he had come to the end of all he wanted the people to hear, he went into Capernaum. ² A centurion there had a servant, a favorite of his, ³ who was sick and near death. ·Having heard about Jesus he sent some Jewish elders to him to ⁴ ask him to come and heal his servant. ·When they came to Jesus they pleaded earnestly with him. ⁵ "He deserves this of you," they said, ·"because he is friendly toward our people; in fact, he is the ⁶ one who built the synagogue." ·So Jesus went with them, and was not very far from the house when the centurion sent word to him by some friends: "Sir," he said, "do not put yourself to trouble; because I am not worthy to have you un- ⁷ der my roof; ·and for this same reason I did not presume to come to you myself; but give the word ⁸ and let my servant be cured. ·For I am under au- thority myself, and have soldiers under me; and I say to one man: Go, and he goes; to another: Come here, and he comes; to my servant: Do ⁹ this, and he does it." ·When Jesus heard these words he was astonished at him and, turning around, said to the crowd following him, "I tell you, not even in Israel have I found faith like ¹⁰ this." ·And when the messengers got back to the house they found the servant in perfect health.

¹¹ Now soon afterward he went to a town called Nain, accompanied by his disciples and a great ¹² number of people. ·When he was near the gate of the town it happened that a dead man was being carried out for burial, the only son of his mother, and she was a widow. And a considerable number ¹³ of the townspeople were with her. ·When the Lord

saw her he felt sorry for her. "Do not cry," he
14 said. ·Then he went up and put his hand on the
bier and the bearers stood still, and he said,
15 "Young man, I tell you to get up." ·And the dead
man sat up and began to talk, and Jesus gave him
16 to his mother. ·Everyone was filled with awe and
praised God saying, "A great prophet has appeared among us; God has visited his people."
17 And this opinion of him spread throughout Judaea
and all over the countryside.

✠

Now that he has detailed Jesus' kingdom preaching
in the Sermon on the Plain (6:17–49), Luke turns to
a description of two miracles of Jesus. In doing so, he
highlights once more who Jesus is and also sets the
stage for John the Baptist's question, "Are you the one
who is to come or have we to wait for someone else?"
(7:20).

The healing of the centurion's servant (7:1–10) is
a strange miracle indeed; the cure is hardly mentioned
at all. The emphases within the story fall on the beneficence (7:5) and especially on the faith (7:9) of the
centurion. This story signals that a non-Jew is worthy
to embrace the benefits issuing from Jesus' kingdom
power. It also points toward the Gentile mission. Is it
coincidental that the first Gentile convert mentioned in
the Acts of the Apostles is a centurion, named Cornelius, who "gave generously to Jewish causes" (Acts
10:2)? Cornelius, like the centurion in our story, has
faith in Jesus although he has never seen him.

By restoring the only son of the widow of Nain to
life (7:11–17), Jesus acts out God's mercy. In Jesus,
God is visiting his people, drawing near to them in their
distress (7:16). See 1:68, "Blessed be the Lord, the

God of Israel, for he has *visited* his people, he has come
to their rescue." Jesus may be likened to the prophet
Elijah, who through prayer restored a widow's son to
life and "gave him to his mother" (7:15; see 1 K
17:23). But he is more. As Lord (7:13), he frees
people from the captivity of death. Through Jesus "the
dead are raised to life" (7:22).

STUDY QUESTION: What is there about the centurion's
faith that merits Jesus' accolade, "I
tell you, not even in Israel have I
found faith like this" (7:9)?

Luke 7:18–35
REVELATION AND REACTION

18 The disciples of John gave him all this news,
19 and John, summoning two of his disciples, ·sent
them to the Lord to ask, "Are you the one who
is to come, or must we wait for someone else?"
20 When the men reached Jesus they said, "John the
Baptist has sent us to you, to ask, 'Are you the
one who is to come or have we to wait for some-
21 one else?' " ·It was just then that he cured many
people of diseases and afflictions and of evil spirits, and gave the gift of sight to many who were
22 blind. ·Then he gave the messengers their answer,
"Go back and tell John what you have seen and
heard: the blind see again, the lame walk, lepers
are cleansed, and the deaf hear, the dead are
raised to life, the Good News is proclaimed to the
23 poor ·and happy is the man who does not lose
faith in me."

24 When John's messengers had gone he began to
25 talk to the people about John, ·"What did you go
out into the wilderness to see? A reed swaying in
the breeze? No? Then what did you go out to see?
A man dressed in fine clothes? Oh no, those who
go in for fine clothes and live luxuriously are to
26 be found at court! ·Then what did you go out to
see? A prophet? Yes, I tell you, and much more
27 than a prophet: ·he is the one of whom scripture
says:

See, I am going to send my messenger before
you;
he will prepare the way before you.

28 "I tell you, of all the children born of women,
there is no one greater than John; yet the least

²⁹ in the kingdom of God is greater than he is." ·All
the people who heard him, and the tax collectors
too, acknowledged God's plan by accepting bap-
³⁰ tism from John; ·but by refusing baptism from
him the Pharisees and the lawyers had thwarted
what God had in mind for them.

³¹   "What description, then, can I find for the men
³² of this generation? What are they like? ·They are
like children shouting to one another while they
sit in the market place:

> 'We played the pipes for you,
>   and you wouldn't dance;
> we sang dirges,
>   and you wouldn't cry.'

³³   "For John the Baptist comes, not eating bread,
not drinking wine, and you say, 'He is possessed.'
³⁴ The Son of Man comes, eating and drinking, and
you say, 'Look, a glutton and a drunkard, a friend
³⁵ of tax collectors and sinners.' ·Yet Wisdom has
been proved right by all her children."

✠

Let's use "reaction" as the code word by which we
can crack the messages of this section.

In prison John hears about Jesus' preaching and miracles and reacts by sending two disciples to ask him
point-blank whether he is the Messiah. Jesus reacts to
John's question by fulfilling, in clear view of John's two
witnesses, the prophecy with which he began his public
ministry (7:21; see 4:18). John will truly be happy if
he rids himself of his opinion that Jesus should be a
Messiah in the finest fire-and-brimstone tradition (see
3:17). John the Baptist and Luke's readers are challenged to rethink their image of God and his Messiah,
Jesus. God is merciful, and Jesus embodies that mercy

by restoring people to health and by preaching God's mercy to the outcasts of society.

After John's disciples return to their master, Jesus reacts to John's ministry and in doing so reveals more about himself. John is a prophet, and surely no one born of women is greater than John, yet he is just the messenger who prepared for God's coming in Jesus (7:27). Although Jesus seemed to be inferior to John because he was baptized by him, he actually is greater than John because he brings God's kingdom (7:28).

The reactions given to the revelation of John the Baptist are like the reactions which befall Jesus' revelation. Whereas the religious leaders of Judaism react negatively to John, all the people and the hated tax collectors react most favorably (7:29–30). John the Baptist and Jesus just couldn't win with the religious leaders. John said, "Let's fast and repent," and they replied that they'd rather eat and drink. Jesus said, "Let's eat and drink and have a good time," and they rejoined that they'd rather fast and repent. The people, the tax collectors, and the sinners are open to the revelation of John and Jesus. They form the nucleus of God's renewed people, and by their reactions to John and Jesus show how truly wise they are.

STUDY QUESTION: Revelation and reaction. Is it possible to become comfortable with a God who loves table fellowship with the scum of society?

Luke 7:36–50
FORGIVENESS ACTED OUT

³⁶ One of the Pharisees invited him to a meal. When he arrived at the Pharisee's house and took ³⁷ his place at table, ·a woman came in, who had a bad name in the town. She had heard he was dining with the Pharisee and had brought with her ³⁸ an alabaster jar of ointment. ·She waited behind him at his feet, weeping, and her tears fell on his feet, and she wiped them away with her hair; then she covered his feet with kisses and anointed them with the ointment.

³⁹ When the Pharisee who had invited him saw this, he said to himself, "If this man were a prophet, he would know who this woman is that is touching him and what a bad name she has." ⁴⁰ Then Jesus took him up and said, "Simon, I have something to say to you." "Speak, Master," was ⁴¹ the reply. ·"There was once a creditor who had two men in his debt; one owed him five hundred ⁴² denarii, the other fifty. ·They were unable to pay, so he pardoned them both. Which of them will ⁴³ love him more?" ·"The one who was pardoned more, I suppose," answered Simon. Jesus said, "You are right."

⁴⁴ Then he turned to the woman. "Simon," he said, "you see this woman? I came into your house, and you poured no water over my feet, but she has poured out her tears over my feet and ⁴⁵ wiped them away with her hair. ·You gave me no kiss, but she has been covering my feet with kisses ⁴⁶ ever since I came in. ·You did not anoint my head with oil, but she has anointed my feet with oint- ⁴⁷ ment. ·For this reason I tell you that her sins, her many sins, must have been forgiven her, or she

would not have shown such great love. It is the man who is forgiven little who shows little love."

48 Then he said to her, "Your sins are forgiven."

49 Those who were with him at table began to say to themselves, "Who is this man, that he even for-

50 gives sins?" ·But he said to the woman, "Your faith has saved you; go in peace."

✠

I suppose that most of us have seen a movie which was so powerful that we couldn't grasp its total message in one viewing. We went to see the movie again to spot the things we missed the first time around. This story is like a powerful movie. Before you continue with this commentary, read the story through again. The commentary will show the key scenes in slow motion and allow you to grasp what the story is saying about Jesus, the church, and forgiveness.

The story features Jesus, "friend of tax collectors and sinners" (7:34). Jesus does not share the religious viewpoint which labels mixing with sinners a no-no (7:39). He allows the sinful woman to touch him and to thank him lavishly for forgiving her sins. The God whose kingdom Jesus brings is not a God who restricts his mercy to the righteous and lets sinners rot in their sins. Jesus' mercy toward the sinful woman jars the consciousness of those who sit at table with him: "Who does this fellow think he is, saying he can 'forgive sins'!" (7:49).

This is the first of three stories in which Jesus dines with a Pharisee (see also 11:37–54 and 14:1–24). Unlike those other accounts, where the Pharisees argue with Jesus about a point of law, here the Pharisee is more concerned with the nature of Jesus' mission: How can such a supposedly holy man associate with sinners?

In Luke's eyes the Pharisee is representative of those Christians within his church who haven't been forgiven many sins and view with some apprehension the church's concern for the notoriously sinful. These Pharisees are reminded that Jesus has revealed God as a God of boundless mercy. The church should hesitate before rushing in work crews to erect a fence around that mercy.

It is difficult to fathom the rich interrelationships between the words "forgiveness," "love," and "faith" in verses 47–50. On one level, the theological problems of these rich interrelationships are solved by seeing that the sinful woman's acts of love flowed from her belief that Jesus had truly offered her God's mercy and forgiveness. On another level, faith saves those who turn from their sins (7:50); they show that they have received forgiveness by their acts of charity and thankfulness (7:47).

STUDY QUESTION: Does this story mean much to Christians today when the notion of sin is in such flux?

Luke 8:1–3
FEMALE FOLLOWERS OF JESUS

8 ¹ Now after this he made his way through towns and villages preaching, and proclaiming the Good News of the kingdom of God. With him ² went the Twelve, ·as well as certain women who had been cured of evil spirits and ailments: Mary surnamed the Magdalene, from whom seven de- ³ mons had gone out, ·Joanna the wife of Herod's steward Chuza, Susanna, and several others who provided for them out of their own resources.

✠

This brief summary is usually skimmed over as a mere introduction to the popular Parable of the Sower (8:4–15). Yet the refrain "kingdom of God" and a glance at Jewish mores at the time of Jesus invite us to see something more in 8:2–3 than mere window dressing.

An accurate generalization about women in Jesus' time would be that they had little social or religious standing. The Jerusalem Temple had a special section (the Court of the Women) beyond which they could not go. They could not become disciples of a rabbi. They should be veiled in public. The rabbis enjoined: "Do not speak much with a woman on the street." Against this background it is striking that Jesus, the bringer of God's kingdom, associated with women and had female followers. In Jesus, God's rule of love is

anything but chauvinistic; it is for both men and
women.

This summary resonates with other sections of
Luke's work. Besides Elisabeth, Mary, and Anna
(chapters 1 and 2), these other women figure in the
Jesus story: Simon's mother-in-law (4:38–39), the
widow at Nain (7:11–17), a sinful woman (7:36–50),
the possessed women (8:2), the woman with the hem-
orrhage (8:43–48), Martha and Mary (10:38–42), a
crippled woman (13:10–17), the widow who gives an
offering (21:1–4), the women at the crucifixion (23:
49, 55), and the women as witnesses to the empty tomb
(24:10–11, 22–23), as well as the women in Jesus'
parables of the woman and the lost coin (15:8–10) and
of the widow and the judge (18:1–8). See also
the mention in Acts 1:14 of women and Mary in the
Jerusalem community. A number of these passages
(7:11–17, 7:36–50, 8:2, 10:38–42, 13:10–17, 15:8–
10, 18:1–8) are only found in Luke's Gospel.

Four key points emerge from Luke's presentation of
Jesus' association with women. First, Jesus goes against
the mores of his time and associates freely with women,
an "outcast" class. Second, he respects their full human
dignity. Third, they are his most faithful followers. Like
the Twelve and the disciples, they witness to what Jesus
says and does during his earthly ministry; but unlike
the Twelve and the disciples, they remain completely
faithful to Jesus when the chips are down (see 23:49,
55). Fourth, they seem to have played an important
role in the church of Luke's time.

STUDY QUESTION: In *Jesus According to a Woman,*
Rachel Conrad Wahlberg asks a
probing question: Why has the
Church been blind to the sig-

nificance of Jesus' association with women? In what ways can the contemporary church follow in the footsteps of the Jesus who respected the full human dignity of women?

Luke 8:4–21
THE KINGDOM OF GOD
THROUGH MATURE EYES

4   With a large crowd gathering and people from every town finding their way to him, he used this parable:

5   "A sower went out to sow his seed. As he sowed, some fell on the edge of the path and was trampled on; and the birds of the air ate it up.

6 Some seed fell on rock, and when it came up it

7 withered away, having no moisture. ·Some seed fell among thorns and the thorns grew with it

8 and choked it. ·And some seed fell into rich soil and grew and produced its crop a hundredfold." Saying this he cried, "Listen, anyone who has ears to hear!"

9   His disciples asked him what this parable might

10 mean, ·and he said, "The mysteries of the kingdom of God are revealed to you; for the rest there are only parables, so that

> they may see but not perceive,
> listen but not understand.

11   "This, then, is what the parable means: the seed

12 is the word of God. ·Those on the edge of the path are people who have heard it, and then the devil comes and carries away the word from their hearts in case they should believe and be saved.

13 Those on the rock are people who, when they first hear it, welcome the word with joy. But these have no root; they believe for a while, and in time of

14 trial they give up. ·As for the part that fell into thorns, this is people who have heard, but as they go on their way they are choked by the worries and

riches and pleasures of life and do not reach ma-
15 turity. ·As for the part in the rich soil, this is people with a noble and generous heart who have
heard the word and take it to themselves and yield
a harvest through their perseverance.

16   "No one lights a lamp to cover it with a bowl or
to put it under a bed. No, he puts it on a lampstand so that people may see the light when they
17 come in. ·For nothing is hidden but it will be made
clear, nothing secret but it will be known and
18 brought to light. ·So take care how you hear; for
anyone who has will be given more; from anyone
who has not, even what he thinks he has will be
taken away."

19   His mother and his brothers came looking for
him, but they could not get to him because of the
20 crowd. ·He was told, "Your mother and brothers
21 are standing outside and want to see you." ·But he
said in answer, "My mother and my brothers are
those who hear the word of God and put it into
practice."

✠

Imagine yourself asking two people, one aged twenty
and the other aged seventy, to read a great piece of
literature like *War and Peace*. After they have read the
masterpiece, you then ask them to interpret the story
for you in terms of their own life experience. I would
venture to say that the seventy-year-old would have a
richer understanding of the book's message.

The above exercise in imagination sets us on our way
to uncovering the meaning of this section. The great
piece of literature is "the kingdom of God" which Jesus
preaches and brings (see 8:1). The word of God is that
God's rule is merciful (8:11). Despite the apparent dis-
aster of rock and thorn, that word will yield a super-
abundant harvest (8:4–8).

The church, as it beds down with Jesus' message of God's kingdom, can be likened to the seventy-year-old. Since its members have been given knowledge of the secrets of the kingdom of God (8:10), they continue to preach that God's rule is merciful and that Jesus makes God's rule present. They cannot keep the kingdom message hidden under a bed (8:16). The kingdom of God is God's word for them. The experience of age has taught Luke's community that the word, once believed, leads to salvation (8:12). Experience has also advised them that the trials of persecution are going to swoop down on them. The worries and riches and pleasures of this present life are going to gnaw at their faith and erode their membership rolls. The rich harvest of faith is for those who persevere (8:15). Truly, the Christians of Luke's time must take care how they hear God's word (8:18). They will be mothers and brothers to Jesus provided they "hear the word of God and put it into practice" (8:21).

In powerfully moving words Jesus told the story that God's rule is merciful and that setbacks are only apparent and will not detour that rule from triumphing. Some fifty years after the death of Jesus the church of Luke's time has the rich experience of age to fathom Jesus' story. While its missionary endeavors may meet with rejection and even imprisonment, it, like Paul, continues to proclaim the kingdom of God and to teach the truth about the Lord Jesus Christ (see Ac 28:31).

STUDY QUESTION: Does this section give us any helpful hints on how we should preach and hear the word of God today?

Luke 8:22–56
JESUS' DEEDS AS KEYS
TO THE KINGDOM

22 One day, he got into a boat with his disciples
and said to them, "Let us cross over to the other
23 side of the lake." So they put to sea, ·and as they
sailed he fell asleep. When a squall came down on
the lake the boat started taking in water and they
24 found themselves in danger. ·So they went to
rouse him saying, "Master! Master! We are going
down!" Then he woke up and rebuked the wind
and the rough water; and they subsided and it was
25 calm again. ·He said to them, "Where is your
faith?" They were awestruck and astonished and
said to one another, "Who can this be, that gives
orders even to winds and waves and they obey
him?"

26 They came to land in the country of the Gera-
27 senes, which is opposite Galilee. ·He was stepping
ashore when a man from the town who was possessed by devils came toward him; for a long time
the man had worn no clothes, nor did he live in a
house, but in the tombs.

28 Catching sight of Jesus he gave a shout, fell at
his feet and cried out at the top of his voice,
"What do you want with me, Jesus, son of the
Most High God? I implore you, do not torture
29 me." ·—For Jesus had been telling the unclean
spirit to come out of the man. It was a devil that
had seized on him a great many times, and then
they used to secure him with chains and fetters to
restrain him, but he would always break the fas-
tenings, and the devil would drive him out into the
30 wilds. ·"What is your name?" Jesus asked. "Legion," he said—because many devils had gone into

31 him. ·And these pleaded with him not to order
them to depart into the Abyss.

32   Now there was a large herd of pigs feeding
there on the mountain, and the devils pleaded
with him to let them go into these. So he gave
33 them leave. ·The devils came out of the man and
went into the pigs, and the herd charged down the
cliff into the lake and were drowned.

34   When the swineherds saw what had happened
they ran off and told their story in the town and
35 in the country around about; ·and the people went
out to see what had happened. When they came to
Jesus they found the man from whom the devils
had gone out sitting at the feet of Jesus, clothed
36 and in his full senses; and they were afraid. ·Those
who had witnessed it told them how the man who
37 had been possessed came to be healed. ·The entire
population of the Gerasene territory was in a state
of panic and asked Jesus to leave them. So he got
into the boat and went back.

38   The man from whom the devils had gone out
asked to be allowed to stay with him, but he sent
39 him away. ·"Go back home," he said, "and report
all that God has done for you." So the man went
off and spread throughout the town all that Jesus
had done for him.

40   On his return Jesus was welcomed by the crowd,
41 for they were all there waiting for him. ·And now
there came a man named Jairus, who was an official of the synagogue. He fell at Jesus' feet and
42 pleaded with him to come to his house, ·because
he had an only daughter about twelve years old,
who was dying. And the crowds were almost
stifling Jesus as he went.

43   Now there was a woman suffering from a hem-
orrhage for twelve years, whom no one had been
44 able to cure. ·She came up behind him and
touched the fringe of his cloak; and the hemor-
45 rhage stopped at that instant. ·Jesus said, "Who
touched me?" When they all denied that they had,
Peter and his companions said, "Master, it is the
46 crowds around you, pushing." ·But Jesus said,

"Somebody touched me. I felt that power had gone
47 out from me." ·Seeing herself discovered, the
woman came forward trembling, and falling at his
feet explained in front of all the people why she
had touched him and how she had been cured at
48 that very moment. ·"My daughter," he said, "your
faith has restored you to health; go in peace."
49   While he was still speaking, someone arrived
from the house of the synagogue official to say,
"Your daughter has died. Do not trouble the
50 Master any further." ·But Jesus had heard this,
and he spoke to the man, "Do not be afraid, only
51 have faith and she will be safe." ·When he came to
the house he allowed no one to go in with him
except Peter and John and James, and the child's
52 father and mother. ·They were all weeping and
mourning for her, but Jesus said, "Stop crying; she
53 is not dead, but asleep." ·But they laughed at him,
54 knowing she was dead. ·But taking her by the hand
55 he called to her, "Child, get up." ·And her spirit
returned and she got up at once. Then he told
56 them to give her something to eat. ·Her parents
were astonished, but he ordered them not to tell
anyone what had happened.

✠

There are a number of ways of surveying land. One
is to size up the overall lay of the land—its terrain,
ponds, trees, etc. Another is to make specific probes
in some areas for more detailed information about soil
content, water level, etc. In our survey of this section
we will first take an overall look at the land of these
four miracles stories. Then, we'll make some specific
probes in the areas of Christian mission and faith.

The kingdom of God is God's word (8:11). And it
is more. God's rule relieves distress (8:22–25), expels
demons (8:26–39), cures illness and restores life
(8:40–56). But as we have often reflected in this com-

mentary, that kingdom is not some abstract concept
soaring in an intellectual stratosphere. God's kingdom
is brought about by the historical person Jesus of Nazareth. With the storm raging about him, Jesus shows that
he has the same power attributed to God in the Old
Testament. As the psalmist confessed: "Then they
called to Yahweh in their trouble and he rescued them
from their sufferings, reducing the storm to a whisper
until the waves grew quiet, bringing them, glad at the
calm, safe to the port they were bound for" (Ps 107:28–
30). Jesus not only has power over one or another
demon but actually dominates legion and their dwelling
place, the Abyss (8:31). The Book of Revelation helps
us catch the flavor of Jesus' power over the dreadful
Abyss when the seer says: "Then I saw an angel come
down from heaven with the key of the Abyss in his hand
and an enormous chain. He overpowered the dragon,
that primeval serpent which is the devil and Satan, and
. . . threw him into the Abyss . . ." (Rv 20:1–3). Jesus also saves people from illness (8:48) and death
(8:54–55). The kingdom of God pulses through Jesus'
veins with such intensity that his mere commands are
enough to restore order to the chaos of nature and to
stop demons from harassing humankind with illness
(8:25, 31). This broad and sweeping survey shows that
at the center of the mysteries of the kingdom of God
(8:10) stand Jesus and his kingdom message and deeds.

If we make a specific probe into the story of the Gerasene demoniac (8:26–39), we can spy beneath the sur-
face the future missionary activity of the church. The
Jesus under whose kingdom label the church operates
even has authority over demons in non-Jewish territory.
The salvation from the power of evil which Jesus effects
is for all people. God is so at work in Jesus that when
the healed demoniac is told, "Go back home and report

all that God has done for you," he goes off and spreads throughout the town all that *Jesus* had done for him (8:39).

Let's make a final probe in our surveying efforts and detect the levels of teaching on the role of faith (8:25, 48, 50). The powers of God's rule, unleashed in Jesus' deeds, do not act in a vacuum. They call for and thrive on faith. Caught in the waves of persecution and tossed by the winds of wealth and pleasures (8:13–14), the disciples must increase their faith in the Jesus who will act to calm their stormy lives (8:22–25). Bumping into Jesus in the street will not save anyone; one must have faith that Jesus conveys God's power to cure (8:48). Faith is not a static reality; changed circumstances call for a deepening of that faith (8:50).

STUDY QUESTION: Is it very evident today that God's rule relieves distress, expels demons, cures illness, and restores life?

Luke 9:1–9
DOES JESUS HAVE A FUTURE?

9 ¹ He called the Twelve together and gave them power and authority over all devils and to cure ² diseases, ·and he sent them out to proclaim the ³ kingdom of God and to heal. ·He said to them, "Take nothing for the journey; neither staff, nor haversack, nor bread, nor money; and let none of ⁴ you take a spare tunic. ·Whatever house you enter, stay there; and when you leave, let it be from there. ⁵ As for those who do not welcome you, when you leave their town shake the dust from your feet as ⁶ a sign to them." ·So they set out and went from village to village proclaiming the Good News and healing everywhere.

⁷ Meanwhile Herod the tetrarch had heard about all that was going on; and he was puzzled, because some people were saying that John had risen from ⁸ the dead, ·others that Elijah had reappeared, still others that one of the ancient prophets had come ⁹ back to life. ·But Herod said, "John? I beheaded him. So who is this I hear such reports about?" And he was anxious to see him.

✠

When a business firm comes to the end of its fiscal year, it tallies the year's assets and debits and makes forecasts for the future. Does the future spell expansion, belt-tightening, or possible bankruptcy?

In 9:1–50 Jesus completes his Galilean ministry. The instructions on the top of the tally sheet for the Jesus firm have one question: "Who is this I hear such reports about?" (9:9; contrast Mk 6:16). The success of Jesus' powerful proclamation of the kingdom of God in word and deed (8:1–56) and of the Twelve's similar proclamation (9:1–6, 10) are the immediate occasions for the question. As Herod tallies Jesus' record, he responds to the question like a curiosity seeker: "Let me see him sometime and then I'll give you a more definite answer" (9:9; see 23:8–12). The tally of Peter, Jesus' longtime associate, is that he is "the Christ of God" (9:20). God, whose kingdom Jesus brings, voices the authoritative tally: "This is my Son, the Chosen One" (9:35). But the seemingly dominant forecast in 9:1–50 is that the future of the Jesus firm is bleak. Buyers don't want its product: "The Son of Man is destined to suffer grievously, to be rejected by the elders and chief priests and scribes and to be put to death" (9:22). Jesus may be the Messiah of God and God's Son, but he has no long-term staying power.

Although this pessimistic prognostication of the future of the Jesus firm seems to carry the day, it is only a minority report. Jesus will "be raised up on the third day" (9:22). The Twelve, who form the foundation of God's renewed people, will continue Jesus' kingdom proclamation (9:1–6). Yet the minority report has some truth on its side. The cross will also cast its shadow over the church's later missionary work. As it carries out its missionary work amidst persecution and in pagan lands, the church will have to devise new strategies to replace those of the peaceful days (9:3; see 22:35–38 and the commentary on 10:1–24).

STUDY QUESTIONS: What is your educated guess about the future of the Jesus firm? Do you see yourself playing a role in its future?

Luke 9:10-17
JESUS BRINGS SUSTENANCE

[10] On their return the apostles gave him an account of all they had done. Then he took them with him and withdrew to a town called Bethsaida [11] where they could be by themselves. ·But the crowds got to know and they went after him. He made them welcome and talked to them about the kingdom of God; and he cured those who were in need of healing.

[12] It was late afternoon when the Twelve came to him and said, "Send the people away, and they can go to the villages and farms around about to find lodging and food; for we are in a lonely place [13] here." ·He replied, "Give them something to eat yourselves." But they said, "We have no more than five loaves and two fish, unless we are to go [14] ourselves and buy food for all these people." ·For there were about five thousand men. But he said to his disciples, "Get them to sit down in parties of [15] about fifty." ·They did so and made them all sit [16] down. ·Then he took the five loaves and the two fish, raised his eyes to heaven, and said the blessing over them; then he broke them and handed them to his disciples to distribute among the crowd. [17] They all ate as much as they wanted, and when the scraps remaining were collected they filled twelve baskets.

✠

Those of us who lived in Chicago while Richard J. Daley was mayor know that he sometimes answered the questions of reporters with a story. When reporters

asked him about the trouble a certain political figure
had brought down upon his head by a clumsy statement,
His Honor proceeded to tell them a story about the large
fish he had recently caught while fishing in Lake Michi-
gan. The reporters were annoyed and thought that
Daley was evading their question until he meandered
to the punch line: "You know, if that fish hadn't opened
its mouth, it wouldn't have been caught."

Like reporters, we come to Luke with our question,
"Who is this I hear such reports about?" (9:9). Instead
of giving us a direct answer in this section, Luke tells
us a story. The story answers our question with the refrain "kingdom of God," and with the number twelve
(9:12, 17). The kingdom of God, which Jesus brings,
gives nourishment for his people much like the manna
God gave to his starving people in the desert (see Ex
16:15–16). The Twelve bear witness to the richness of
this food, and their helpers, the disciples (9:14, 16),
distribute it to the people. In its superabundance
of twelve baskets (9:17), it is food for the renewed
Israel, built upon the foundation of the Twelve. And
the words "he said the blessing over them; then he broke
them and handed them to his disciples" (9:16) prompt
the reader to look beyond this food to the Eucharist,
which is for all (9:17; see 22:19 and 24:30).

Luke has answered our question with a captivating
story. Jesus provides nourishment for those who heed
his kingdom message; he continues to nurture his people through the breaking of bread in the Eucharist.

STUDY QUESTION: How does Jesus provide sustenance
for his contemporary followers?

Luke 9:18–27
JESUS TEACHES THE TRUTH
THAT THE MESSIAH MUST SUFFER

18 Now one day when he was praying alone in the presence of his disciples he put this question to
19 them, "Who do the crowds say I am?" ·And they answered, "John the Baptist; others Elijah; and others say one of the ancient prophets come back
20 to life." ·"But you," he said, "who do you say I am?" It was Peter who spoke up. "The Christ of
21 God," he said. ·But he gave them strict orders not to tell anyone anything about this.
22 "The Son of Man," he said, "is destined to suffer grievously, to be rejected by the elders and chief priests and scribes and to be put to death, and to be raised up on the third day."
23 Then to all he said, "If anyone wants to be a follower of mine, let him renounce himself and
24 take up his cross every day and follow me. ·For anyone who wants to save his life will lose it; but anyone who loses his life for my sake, that man
25 will save it. ·What gain, then, is it for a man to have won the whole world and to have lost or
26 ruined his very self? ·For if anyone is ashamed of me and of my words, of him the Son of Man will be ashamed when he comes in his own glory and in the glory of the Father and the holy angels.
27 "I tell you truly, there are some standing here who will not taste death before they see the kingdom of God."

✠

I suppose that most of us have had good teachers who penned detailed comments on papers we had written for them. The teacher counseled that while what we had written was true, it did not go deep enough into the area under consideration. The teacher shared insights on how we could delve deeper into the subject and get a firmer grasp on truth.

In this section Peter's answer that Jesus is "the Christ of God" (9:20) is indeed true. But it is not the whole truth. Jesus, like a good teacher, advises Peter how he can probe deeper into the truth. Jesus' role as Messiah of God must include suffering (9:22). This has been destined by God. Or as the Risen Lord instructs the disciples on the way to Emmaus: "Was it not ordained that the Christ should suffer and so enter into his glory?" (24:26). The truth that Jesus is the suffering Messiah of God has vast implications for all who profess it (9:23–25). If their confession of Jesus as the Messiah of God is to make any sense, they must shoulder their cross every day. Dying to one's self-centeredness for the sake of Jesus is the disciple's way of life. It will take disciples a lifetime of commitment to fathom the truth that Jesus is God's suffering Messiah.

Verse 26 gives further insight into this truth by applying it to the martyrs within Luke's community. Failure to acknowledge Jesus will have dire consequences at the judgment. Verse 27 picks up the refrain "kingdom of God," rounds off this section, and leads into the account of the Transfiguration (9:28–36). In Jesus, God has shown the graciousness of his rule. In the Transfiguration some will see the glory of God's kingdom reflected in Jesus' person. Some will see God's rule over death manifested in Jesus' glorified body. Some, like the

martyr Stephen, will experience the graciousness of
God's rule before their death (see Ac 7:55–56).

STUDY QUESTION: Is your idea of daily cross-bearing
                for Jesus' sake the same today as
                it was ten or fifteen years ago?

Luke 9:28–36
THE TRANSFIGURATION
DISCLOSES WHO JESUS IS

28 Now about eight days after this had been said, he took with him Peter and John and James and
29 went up the mountain to pray. ·As he prayed, the aspect of his face was changed and his clothing
30 became brilliant as lightning. ·Suddenly there were two men there talking to him; they were
31 Moses and Elijah ·appearing in glory, and they were speaking of his passing which he was to ac-
32 complish in Jerusalem. ·Peter and his companions were heavy with sleep, but they kept awake and saw his glory and the two men standing with him.
33 As these were leaving him, Peter said to Jesus, "Master, it is wonderful for us to be here; so let us make three tents, one for you, one for Moses and one for Elijah."—He did not know what he was
34 saying. ·As he spoke, a cloud came and covered them with shadow; and when they went into the
35 cloud the disciples were afraid. ·And a voice came from the cloud saying, "This is my Son, the
36 Chosen One. Listen to him." ·And after the voice had spoken, Jesus was found alone. The disciples kept silence and, at that time, told no one what they had seen.

✠

All of us have disclosed who we are to someone at some time or another. On a vacation we disclosed ourselves when we insisted on driving eight hundred miles a day through the most scenic part of our country with-

out stopping to contemplate the grandeur of it all. Or
we disclosed our love for another person by expressing
the inexpressible through images: "Your smile is the
rudder of my life. Your words cheer my day like a brilliant sunrise."

The Transfiguration is a disclosure of who Jesus is.
To express the inexpressible, Luke uses imagery drawn
from the Old Testament. A verse-by-verse commentary
will provide lookout points for contemplating Jesus'
grandeur.

9:28 The startling truth that Jesus is a suffering Messiah (9:18–27) is closely linked to Jesus' disclosure,
which occurs on a mountain—a traditional place
for revelation/disclosure.

9:29 As Jesus is radiant with the heavenly world,
we recall the description of Moses: "When Moses came
down from the mountain of Sinai . . . he did not know
that the skin of his face was radiant after speaking with
Yahweh" (Ex 34:29).

9:30–31 The epitomes of God's Old Testament revelation in law and prophetic utterance converse with Jesus, who is going to fulfill all their expectations by his
"exodus" ("exodus" is a more literal translation than
"passing"). Through his death, resurrection, and ascension Jesus leads his people in a new exodus from bond-
age to life.

9:32 Whereas Moses reflected God's glory (Ex
34:29), Jesus' glory is his own. That is, God's majesty
and power are visibly present in Jesus.

9:33 In calling for the erection of three tents, Peter

senses the presence of God and wants to capture it. But he misses the point. God's presence is to be found in Jesus' word (see 9:35).

9:34–36   The cloud signifies the presence of God as in Exodus 40:34: "The cloud covered the Tent of Meeting and the glory of Yahweh filled the tabernacle." With greater authority than Moses and Elijah, God confirms the truth of what Jesus had announced in 9:18–27. God underlines in words what was disclosed in the Transfiguration, while the Transfiguration discloses the meaning of the words. The Lord Jesus will be present to his church in his word.

Through the Transfiguration Jesus discloses that the cross will not write the final word to the story of his life. "Was it not ordained that the Christ should suffer and so enter into his glory?" (24:26).

STUDY QUESTION: What does Jesus' self-disclosure in the Transfiguration contribute to our image of him?

Luke 9:37–50
THE TRUTH WHICH REVOLUTIONIZES
HEART AND MIND

37 Now on the following day when they were
coming down from the mountain a large crowd
38 came to meet him. ·Suddenly a man in the crowd
cried out. "Master," he said, "I implore you to
39 look at my son: he is my only child. ·All at once
a spirit will take hold of him, and give a sudden
cry and throw the boy into convulsions with
foaming at the mouth; it is slow to leave him, but
40 when it does it leaves the boy worn out. ·I begged
your disciples to cast it out, and they could not."
41 "Faithless and perverse generation!" Jesus said in
reply. "How much longer must I be among you
42 and put up with you? Bring your son here." ·The
boy was still moving toward Jesus when the devil
threw him to the ground in convulsions. But Jesus
rebuked the unclean spirit and cured the boy and
43 gave him back to his father, ·and everyone was
awestruck by the greatness of God.
     At a time when everyone was full of admiration
44 for all he did, he said to his disciples, ·"For your
part, you must have these words constantly in
your mind: The Son of Man is going to be handed
45 over into the power of men." ·But they did not
understand him when he said this; it was hidden
from them so that they should not see the meaning
of it, and they were afraid to ask him about what
he had just said.
46 An argument started between them about which
47 of them was the greatest. ·Jesus knew what
thoughts were going through their minds, and he
48 took a little child and set him by his side, ·and

then said to them, "Anyone who welcomes this little child in my name welcomes me; and anyone who welcomes me welcomes the one who sent me. For the least among you all, that is the one who is great."

49 John spoke up. "Master," he said, "we saw a man casting out devils in your name, and because
50 he is not with us we tried to stop him." ·But Jesus said to him, "You must not stop him: anyone who is not against you is for you."

✠

The truth that Jesus is a suffering Messiah is not a simple truth like "One plus one equals two," something which can be grasped quickly. It's more like the truth "It is in giving that we receive," which takes a long time, perhaps even a lifetime, to assimilate.

"Everyone was awestruck by the greatness of God" which Jesus manifested in his cure of the demoniac (9:37–43). As they buzzed about the marvels of Jesus' Galilean ministry, "everyone was full of admiration" (9:43). But being awestruck and full of admiration only grant waiting room in the lobby of the truth of who Jesus is.

It is easy for the disciples to join ranks with the crowd and play hooky from reflecting more profoundly on Jesus' truth. They are policed back to school by a reminder of Jesus' rejection and cross (9:44). It will take many wrestlings of faith before that truth will dawn on them (9:45). As a matter of fact, they shy away from such a struggle and busily jockey for positions as if they worked for a firm of an earthly messiah. They must learn that a title on their door does not rate them red-carpet treatment. In Jesus' firm, greatness is synonymous with being a premier servant of the helpless (9:46–48). They must avoid the discrimination of making ministry their private club (9:49–50).

Jesus' Galilean ministry is over. Luke presents Jesus as one who wanted to be understood on his own terms— a wish which was never fully honored. The truth he preached and lived even escaped his disciples. But it abides as a challenge for Luke's readers and all their latter-day kin.

STUDY QUESTION: Why does it take so long for Christians to grasp the truth that Jesus is a suffering Messiah?

The Way to Jerusalem:
Instructions for Jesus' Followers
Luke 9:51 to 19:44

Luke 9:51 opens the door to one of Luke's most signal creations, the narrative of Jesus' journey to Jerusalem (9:51 to 19:44). Around some fifteen references to Jesus' journey, Luke has assembled some of the most beloved texts in all the Scriptures—e.g., the parables of the Good Samaritan and the Prodigal Son. The heading given above for these chapters gives us a preview of the significance of Luke's creation.

In 9:51 to 19:44, Luke plays on the various theological meanings of journey. Jesus' teachings reveal God's way (see 10:21-24). When Jesus visits, the Lord himself visits (9:53, 10:1, 19:44; see 7:16). The coming of Jesus brings salvation to those who accept him (19:9).

In depicting Jesus' way as a way to Jerusalem, Luke is not primarily concerned with the historical city Jerusalem. He views Jerusalem as the culmination of God's choicest blessings, as the guardian of God's temple, as the bridge between the past of God's promises and the present of longed-for fulfillment, as the center of the Jewish religious authorities. Jerusalem is also the site of Jesus' confrontation with and rejection by these authorities—the place of his final teachings, his passion and death. It is also the scene of his resurrection and ascension. There the promised Spirit descends upon the 120. From there God continues Jesus' mission in the Way which is the Christian religion (see Ac 9:2, 18:26,

24:22). Jerusalem illumines all of Jesus' teaching in this section much like the denouement of a story casts light on all the preceding elements. Since the religious authorities reject Jesus in Jerusalem, it seems that Jesus' teachings, all the way from Galilee to Jerusalem (see 23:5), have not revealed God's way. But God does not allow these authorities to spell the end of Jesus' way.

As Jesus goes his way to Jerusalem, he is accompanied by his apostles and disciples. The instructions and warnings which Jesus gives to them about mission, prayer, persecution, poor and rich, etc., are meant for the Christians of Luke's own time—the members of the Way. Jesus' apostles are witnesses of his teaching and will be able to preserve it in the new Way after his resurrection (see Ac 1:21–22). No, the rejection of Jesus by the religious authorities in Jerusalem did not invalidate his teaching. God put his stamp of approval on Jesus' way by raising him from the dead and by establishing the new Way in Jerusalem.

For the convenience of the reader we divide the long travel narrative into sections: 9:51 to 13:21, 13:22 to 17:10, and 17:11 to 19:44. The verse which begins each one of these sections explicitly mentions that Jesus is journeying to Jerusalem.

Luke 9:51–62
THE COST OF FOLLOWING JESUS

⁵¹　Now as the time drew near for him to be taken up to heaven, he resolutely took the road for Jeru-
⁵² salem ·and sent messengers ahead of him. These set out, and they went into a Samaritan village to
⁵³ make preparations for him, ·but the people would not receive him because he was making for Jeru-
⁵⁴ salem. ·Seeing this, the disciples James and John said, "Lord, do you want us to call down fire from
⁵⁵ heaven to burn them up?" ·But he turned and re-
⁵⁶ buked them, ·and they went off to another village.
⁵⁷　As they traveled along they met a man on the road who said to him, "I will follow you wherever
⁵⁸ you go." ·Jesus answered, "Foxes have holes and the birds of the air have nests, but the Son of Man has nowhere to lay his head."
⁵⁹　Another to whom he said, "Follow me," re-
⁶⁰ plied, "Let me go and bury my father first." ·But he answered, "Leave the dead to bury their dead; your duty is to go and spread the news of the king-dom of God."
⁶¹　Another said, "I will follow you, sir, but first let me go and say good-by to my people at home."
⁶² Jesus said to him, "Once the hand is laid on the plow, no one who looks back is fit for the king-dom of God."

✠

When Jesus opened his Galilean journey, he suffered rejection (4:16–30). Similarly, he and his disciples en-counter rejection on the first leg of their new journey to Jerusalem (9:52–56). Part of the cost of following

Jesus on his way is the dual realization that not all people are open to the visitation of God's messenger and
that these unreceptive people are not to be feted at a
fire and brimstone display.

The three scenes in 9:57–62 are streamlined. All attention is centered on Jesus' responses. Since the characters of the would-be disciples are left undeveloped,
the Christians of Luke's time can be drawn into the
story line and can identify themselves with them. Jesus'
sayings themselves are veritable show-stoppers. Jesus
does not respond directly to the first person's resolve,
but stops him in his tracks to ponder the consequences
of that resolve. The reasonable requests of the next two
men are bypassed by the admonition to single-
mindedness.

Jesus' sayings clearly focus on the overriding importance of following him. Following him is not a task
which is added to others like working a second job. Nor
is it the earrings or tie-tack stage of dressing up for an
evening out. It is everything. It is a solemn commitment
which forces the disciples-to-be to reorder all their
other duties. The sharpness of Jesus' sayings jars the
readers into weighing most seriously their desire to follow Jesus on his way.

STUDY QUESTION: How practical is it to espouse Jesus'
                  method of value clarification and
                  view one's myriad duties and obliga-
                  tions in the light of the one value
                  of following him?

¹ **10** After this the Lord appointed seventy-two others and sent them out ahead of him, in pairs, to all the towns and places he himself was to ² visit. ·He said to them, "The harvest is rich but the laborers are few, so ask the Lord of the harvest to ³ send laborers to his harvest. ·Start off now, but remember, I am sending you out like lambs among ⁴ wolves. ·Carry no purse, no haversack, no sandals. ⁵ Salute no one on the road. ·Whatever house you go into, let your first words be, 'Peace to this house!' ⁶ And if a man of peace lives there, your peace will go and rest on him; if not, it will come back to ⁷ you. ·Stay in the same house, taking what food and drink they have to offer, for the laborer deserves his wages; do not move from house to ⁸ house. ·Whenever you go into a town where they make you welcome, eat what is set before you. ⁹ Cure those in it who are sick, and say, 'The king- ¹⁰ dom of God is very near to you.' ·But whenever you enter a town and they do not make you wel- ¹¹ come, go out into the streets and say, ·'We wipe off the very dust of your town that clings to our feet, and leave it with you. Yet be sure of this: the ¹² kingdom of God is very near.' ·I tell you, on that day it will not go as hard with Sodom as with that town.

¹³ "Alas for you, Chorazin! Alas for you, Beth-saida! For if the miracles done in you had been done in Tyre and Sidon, they would have repented ¹⁴ long ago, sitting in sackcloth and ashes. ·And still, it will not go as hard with Tyre and Sidon at the ¹⁵ Judgment as with you. ·And as for you, Caper-

naum, did you want to be exalted high as heaven?
You shall be thrown down to hell.

16   "Anyone who listens to you listens to me; anyone who rejects you rejects me, and those who
reject me reject the one who sent me."

17   The seventy-two came back rejoicing. "Lord,"
they said, "even the devils submit to us when we
18 use your name." ·He said to them, "I watched
19 Satan fall like lightning from heaven. ·Yes, I have
given you power to tread underfoot serpents and
scorpions and the whole strength of the enemy;
20 nothing shall ever hurt you. ·Yet do not rejoice
that the Spirits submit to you; rejoice rather that
your names are written in heaven."

21   It was then that, filled with joy by the Holy
Spirit, he said, "I bless you, Father, Lord of
heaven and of earth, for hiding these things from
the learned and the clever and revealing them to
mere children. Yes, Father, for that is what it
22 pleased you to do. ·Everything has been entrusted
to me by my Father; and no one knows who the
Son is except the Father, and who the Father is
except the Son and those to whom the Son chooses
to reveal him."

23   Then turning to his disciples he spoke to them
in private, "Happy the eyes that see what you see,
24 for I tell you that many prophets and kings
wanted to see what you see, and never saw it; to
hear what you hear, and never heard it."

✠

Each word in the heading above touches on a key
idea in this passage. The mission to be continued is
Jesus'. Verses 16, 19, and 21–24 pulsate with some of
the most pregnant christological statements in the Gospel. Their vocabulary may not be that of a Paul Tillich
or of Chalcedon, but it is profound nevertheless. What
the people of the Old Testament longed for is present
in Jesus' deeds and teaching as Jesus, Son of the Father,

reveals God's will and way (10:21–24). As herald of God's kingdom, Jesus overthrows God's enemies, the forces of evil (10:19). When Jesus visits people, the Lord himself visits them (10:1, 16). This is the Jesus whose mission is continued.

The perceptive reader will be quick to recall that during Jesus' Galilean ministry there was a mission of the Twelve (9:1–6, 10–11) and to muse, Why this new mission? The answer lies in the richly symbolic number seventy-two. Genesis 10 numbers the nations of the earth at seventy-two. The Christian mission to all the nations of the earth (see Ac 1:8) is foreshadowed in Jesus' commissioning of the seventy-two. Further, the sending of the seventy-two provides Luke with an opportunity to collect instructions from various sources for the missionaries of his own day (10:2–12). For the most part, these instructions stem from an experience of missionary expansion whose peacefulness enabled Christians to support the missionaries operating in their locale (see 10:4–7).

The seventy-two are not freelance missionaries. They embark on mission under the masthead of Jesus' name and power. " 'Anyone who listens to you listens to me; anyone who rejects you rejects me, and those who reject me reject the one who sent me' " (10:16). In Jesus' name the seventy-two subdue the forces of the enemy (10:17).

The missionary work described in this passage is so vital for his church that Luke alludes to it again. During the Last Supper Jesus asks his disciples, " 'When I sent you out without purse or haversack or sandals, were you short of anything?' 'No,' they said. He said to them, 'But now . . . if you have no sword, sell your cloak and buy one' " (22:35–36). Luke 10:4 is the obvious referent of Jesus' question. The palpable tension between the two passages reflects different missionary experiences. The instructions of 10:4 originate in peaceful missionary endeavor, whereas 22:35–36 issues from the missionary activity of a church which shares the fate of its persecuted Lord.

STUDY QUESTION: What form should Christian mission assume in a world where the vast majority of people are non-Christian?

Luke 10:25-37
A QUESTION OF LAW:
WHO BELONGS TO THE CHURCH?

25 There was a lawyer who, to disconcert him, stood up and said to him, "Master, what must I do 26 to inherit eternal life?" ·He said to him, "What is written in the Law? What do you read there?" 27 He replied, "You must love the Lord your God with all your heart, with all your soul, with all your strength, and with all your mind, and your 28 neighbor as yourself." ·"You have answered right," said Jesus, "do this and life is yours."

29 But the man was anxious to justify himself and 30 said to Jesus, "And who is my neighbor?" ·Jesus replied, "A man was once on his way down from Jerusalem to Jericho and fell into the hands of brigands; they took all he had, beat him and then 31 made off, leaving him half dead. ·Now a priest happened to be traveling down the same road, but when he saw the man, he passed by on the other 32 side. ·In the same way a Levite who came to the place saw him, and passed by on the other side. 33 But a Samaritan traveler who came upon him was 34 moved with compassion when he saw him. ·He went up and bandaged his wounds, pouring oil and wine on them. He then lifted him on to his own mount, carried him to the inn and looked 35 after him. ·Next day, he took out two denarii and handed them to the innkeeper. 'Look after him,' he said, 'and on my way back I will make good 36 any extra expense you have.' ·Which of these three, do you think, proved himself a neighbor to 37 the man who fell into the brigands' hands?" ·"The one who took pity on him," he replied. Jesus said to him, "Go, and do the same yourself."

✠

The heading of this passage may be eyebrow-raising. Doesn't Karris realize that the central point of this passage is the beautiful lesson of social concern taught by the incomparable parable of the Good Samaritan? Oh yes, the commentator knows full well that that parable occurs in this passage. But he maintains that our inherited common parlance has trained us to view that parable almost exclusively in terms of social concern. Recall, for example, the well-worn newspaper headline "Good Samaritan Comes to the Rescue." The interpretation offered here recaptures the mind-twisting function of the parable in a controversy over law, and contends that social concern is a byproduct and not the meat of 10:25–37.

Luke has a habit of interpreting his parables by adding introductions or conclusions to them; for example, he creates a special introduction for the three parables of the lost sheep, coin, and son in chapter 15. In the passage at hand Luke has so artistically added an introduction and conclusion to the parable of the Good Samaritan that the entire passage forms a unity—a controversy story composed of two parallel parts:

1. The lawyer's *question* (10:25)
   Jesus' *counterquestion* (10:26)
   The lawyer's own *answer* (10:27)
   Jesus' *command* (10:28)

2. The lawyer's further *question* (10:29)
   Jesus' *counterquestion* (10:30–36)
   The lawyer's own *answer* (10:37a)
   Jesus' *command* (10:37b)

The passage begins and ends with a question of law. We can specify that question by examining the verses which bracket the parable—verses 29, 36–37.

In verse 29 the lawyer singles out the word "neighbor" from the Old Testament quotations of verses 26–27. His question is born of controversies over membership in God's covenant people and really means, "Who is a member of God's covenant community and therefore an object of my mercy?" In verse 37a the lawyer is forced by Jesus' parable to answer his own question with " 'The one who took pity on him.' " Jesus has gotten the upper hand in his controversy with the lawyer and has turned the lawyer's question on its head. In effect, Jesus says, "Don't search for those who are neighbors, but for those who act like a neighbor." The Samaritan, who doesn't belong by birth to God's covenant people, actually acts like a member of that people by being compassionate. Non-Jews, like the Samaritan, can become members of God's covenant people by showing mercy. Jesus' command in the latter part of verse 37 finalizes his victory in the controversy: Jews can lose their membership in God's covenant community if they do not observe the law of mercy.

The parable of the Good Samaritan functions as part of Luke's answer to a gigantic mission problem in his church: What role does the Law have in saying who's in or out of the church? Luke's answer is revolutionary: The person who observes the covenant law of mercy—be he Jew, Samaritan, or Gentile—is a member of God's church.

STUDY QUESTIONS: What intellectual means do we have of responding to a newfangled interpretation which challenges our time-honored view? If

Luke's answer to the question of law and mission in this passage is complete, what need is there for other entrance requirements, such as baptism?

Luke 10:38–42
THE CHURCH'S MISSION
WELCOMES WOMEN

38 In the course of their journey he came to a village, and a woman named Martha welcomed him
39 into her house. ·She had a sister called Mary, who sat down at the Lord's feet and listened to him
40 speaking. ·Now Martha who was distracted with all the serving said, "Lord, do you not care that my sister is leaving me to do the serving all by my-
41 self? Please tell her to help me.' ·But the Lord answered: "Martha, Martha," he said, "you
42 worry and fret about so many things, ·and yet few are needed, indeed only one. It is Mary who has chosen the better part; it is not to be taken from her."

✠

These five verses are like shale oil, rich in meaning but difficult to recover. Our mining operation begins with some specific comments on individual verses and concludes with a sampling of the riches of the passage.

10:38 Luke again gives notice that Jesus is journeying (to Jerusalem). Jesus, the divine visitor, is welcomed as a guest. This story may also deal with the theme of mission (when Jesus visits, God visits) developed in 10:1–24.

10:39 Mary "sat down at the Lord's feet and listened to him speaking." Jesus is called by his postresurrection title "Lord." The Greek behind "listened to him speaking" is literally translated "listened to his word." Mary is not intent on listening to Jesus' views on the crops and weather. She is all ears to his teaching. The scene is extraordinary. What the rabbis would never do, Jesus does—he has a female disciple.

10:41–42 Few food items are needed. Indeed, if one queries about ultimate foundations, then only one thing is needed. That is the one chosen by Mary—discipleship and following Jesus as the ultimate value in life (see 9:57–62). In the light of discipleship everything else is secondary.

This passage prescribes startling etiquette for entertaining a divine guest. Martha's entertainment plans are subject to the demands of discipleship, which pre-empt all other concerns, even her very legitimate ones (see Ac 6:2). Mary entertains the divine guest by becoming his disciple. Viewed in the context of Luke's missionary teaching in 10:1–24 and 10:25–37, this means that the preaching of the Lord's word is for men and women alike.

STUDY QUESTION: Is it legitimate to see in Martha and Mary general principles for Christian conduct—that is, service (Martha) is subordinate to contemplation and prayer (Mary)?

Luke 11:1–13
PRAYER IN THE MIDST OF TRIAL

¹ 11 Now once he was in a certain place praying, and when he had finished one of his disciples said, "Lord, teach us to pray, just as John taught ² his disciples." ·He said to them, "Say this when you pray:

> 'Father, may your name be held holy,
> Your kingdom come;
> ³ give us each day our daily bread,
> and forgive us our sins,
> ⁴ for we ourselves forgive each one who is in debt
> to us.
> And do not put us to the test.'"

⁵ He also said to them, "Suppose one of you has a friend and goes to him in the middle of the night ⁶ to say, 'My friend, lend me three loaves, ·because a friend of mine on his travels has just arrived at ⁷ my house and I have nothing to offer him'; ·and the man answers from inside the house, 'Do not bother me. The door is bolted now, and my children and I are in bed; I cannot get up to give it ⁸ you.' ·I tell you, if the man does not get up and give it him for friendship's sake, persistence will be enough to make him get up and give his friend all he wants.

⁹ "So I say to you: Ask, and it will be given to you; search, and you will find; knock, and the ¹⁰ door will be opened to you. ·For the one who asks always receives; the one who searches always finds; the one who knocks will always have the ¹¹ door opened to him. ·What father among you would hand his son a stone when he asked for ¹² bread? Or hand him a snake instead of a fish? ·Or

¹³ hand him a scorpion if he asked for an egg? ·If you then, who are evil, know how to give your children what is good, how much more will the heavenly Father give the Holy Spirit to those who ask him!"

✠

As we noted in the Introduction, Luke writes his Gospel for Christians who are faced with persecution and the dual problem this creates, namely, depletion of hope in a God who cares and loss of worldly possessions because of allegiance to Jesus. In this section Luke has masterfully molded three of Jesus' sayings into teaching for these Christians.

For these Christians Jesus is the prime example of prayer (11:1; see also 3:21; 5:16; 6:12; 9:18, 28–29; 22:32, 44; 23:34, 46). Jesus is not the example just because he follows a daily prayer regimen and spends a day or night in prayer before major events. His prayer to his Father enables him to withstand the onslaught of Satan in the midst of the trial of his betrayal, passion, and death (22:44). As Jesus dies a martyr's death, his "Father, into your hands I commit my spirit" evidences his complete trust in his Father (23:46).

If the Christians' prayer is to be heard, it must be persistent (11:5–8; see also 18:1–8). The Christians must ask, search, and knock (11:9–10). In response to persistent prayer, the heavenly Father will not give worldly goods, which might only create additional problems for the persecuted Christians, but the Holy Spirit, who strengthens in persecution (11:13; contrast Mt 7:11). "'When they take you before synagogues and magistrates and authorities, do not worry about how to defend yourselves or what to say, because when the

time comes, the Holy Spirit will teach you what you
must say'" (12:11–12).

These commands to imitate Jesus at prayer and to
pray persistently could breed despair were it not for the
reality behind them. The disciples on Jesus' way experience God as Father because Jesus shares his experience of God-Father with them (11:2). This Father,
who cares deeply for Jesus' followers (11:11–13), will
not put them to that ultimate test wherein they might
fall away (11:4). God is not only imaged as a Father;
he is also friend (11:5–8), who cares for his friends,
the followers of Jesus.

STUDY QUESTIONS: In a difficult situation isn't prayer a
dodge? Why not use one's God-
given talents to resolve the difficulty?

RELENTLESS ADHERENCE TO JESUS

¹⁴ He was casting out a devil and it was dumb; but when the devil had gone out the dumb man spoke, ¹⁵ and the people were amazed. •But some of them said, "It is through Beelzebul, the prince of devils, ¹⁶ that he casts out devils." •Others asked him, as a ¹⁷ test, for a sign from heaven; •but, knowing what they were thinking, he said to them, "Every kingdom divided against itself is heading for ruin, and ¹⁸ a household divided against itself collapses. •So too with Satan: if he is divided against himself, how can his kingdom stand?—Since you assert that ¹⁹ it is through Beelzebul that I cast out devils. •Now if it is through Beelzebul that I cast out devils, through whom do your own experts cast them ²⁰ out? Let them be your judges, then. •But if it is through the finger of God that I cast out devils, then know that the kingdom of God has over-²¹ taken you. •So long as a strong man fully armed guards his own palace, his goods are undisturbed; ²² but when someone stronger than he is attacks and defeats him, the stronger man takes away all the weapons he relied on and shares out his spoil.

²³ "He who is not with me is against me; and he who does not gather with me scatters.

²⁴ "When an unclean spirit goes out of a man it wanders through waterless country looking for a place to rest, and not finding one it says, 'I will go ²⁵ back to the home I came from.' •But on arrival, ²⁶ finding it swept and tidied, •it then goes off and brings seven other spirits more wicked than itself, and they go in and set up house there, so that the man ends up by being worse than he was before."

²⁷ Now as he was speaking, a woman in the crowd

raised her voice and said, "Happy the womb that
28 bore you and the breasts you sucked!" ·But he
replied, "Still happier those who hear the word of
God and keep it!"

29   The crowds got even bigger and he addressed
them, "This is a wicked generation; it is asking
for a sign. The only sign it will be given is the sign
30 of Jonah. ·For just as Jonah became a sign to the
Ninevites, so will the Son of Man be to this gener-
31 ation. ·On Judgment day the Queen of the South
will rise up with the men of this generation and
condemn them, because she came from the ends
of the earth to hear the wisdom of Solomon; and
32 there is something greater than Solomon here. ·On
Judgment day the men of Nineveh will stand up
with this generation and condemn it, because
when Jonah preached they repented; and there is
something greater than Jonah here.

33   "No one lights a lamp and puts it in some
hidden place or under a tub, but on the lampstand
so that people may see the light when they come
34 in. ·The lamp of your body is your eye. When your
eye is sound, your whole body too is filled with
light; but when it is diseased your body too will be
35 all darkness. ·See to it then that the light inside you
36 is not darkness. ·If, therefore, your whole body is
filled with light, and no trace of darkness, it will
be light entirely, as when the lamp shines on you
with its rays."

✠

This section sports verses which have puzzled readers
for ages—11:24–26 and 11:33–36. The pieces of the
puzzle of these verses may fall together if we set them
within the larger context of 11:14–36, where Luke has
fashioned traditional materials about Jesus into additional instructions for his persecuted church. After con-
centrating on specific verses, we will give an overall
view of Luke's message.

11:15–16 Not only the religious leaders, the scribes and Pharisees (see 6:11 and 11:53–54), oppose Jesus; ordinary folk join in the fray. Opposition to Christians will issue from leaders and common people. Luke molds a unity out of the different materials in this section by having Jesus answer the opposition of 11:15 in 11:17–28 whereas the objection of 11:16 is first answered in 11:29–36.

11:20–22 These verses stress the signal meaning of Jesus for Christians. Jesus' exorcisms evidence that God acts in and through him, just as he worked through Moses during the ten plagues of Egypt. See Exodus 8:15, where the phrase "the finger of God" is found in the account of the plagues. Jesus is the stronger one, who has defeated the prince of devils. That Jesus has conquered the evil spirit and that his followers receive the Holy Spirit (11:13) is a tremendous source of consolation for Luke's beleaguered church.

11:23–28 In a life-or-death situation Christians cannot detour from Jesus' way (11:23). Following upon the exorcism of the devil from their lives, they cannot be content merely to sweep and tidy their persons, but they must also welcome Jesus as their permanent house guest. If they try to remain neutral, a whole army (the number seven means fullness) of unwelcome guests will descend upon them and take control. Surely, a worse state results (11:24–26). How can Christians adhere to Jesus in such a do-or-die situation where the opposition forces are so numerous and strong? Their strength lies in the Word of God, which they must hear and keep (11:27–28; see also 8:19–21).

11:29–32 This passage builds upon the objection

raised in 11:16. No spellbinding sign will be given po-
tential converts. The message preached to them, as it
had been to converts before them, is the awesomely
simple *Repent*. Jesus, whom the church preaches, is a
greater sage than Solomon and a greater prophet than
Jonah. The pagan Queen of the South and the pagan
Ninevites show how one must respond to Jesus. Repentance is continually called for (see 11:23–28).

11:33–36   Verses 34–36 have been added to verse 33,
which Luke had previously used in 8:16. The key
clause in 11:33 is the uniquely Lukan "when they come
in." Contrast the parallel verses in Mark and Matthew:

> "Would you bring in a lamp to put it under a
> tub or under the bed? Surely you will put it on
> the lampstand?" (Mk 4:21).

> "No one lights a lamp to put it under a tub; they
> put it on the lampstand where it shines for
> everyone in the house" (Mt 5:15).

Luke's addition to this traditional saying refers to the
light of the Christian mission which is to be lit to be
seen by those who enter the church—not extinguished
at the first muttering of opposition. Luke 11:34–36 follows upon this admonition and stresses the soundness
or singleness of the eye (11:34). When the eye is
sound, then there is single-minded dedication to the
light of the Christian mission. The sound eye results
from relentless adherence to Jesus and enables the
Christian to view all of reality from the elemental perspective of the Lord Jesus.

Just as Jesus experienced opposition from numerous

types of foes, so too will his church. Luke exhorts his fellow Christians to draw strength and consolation from Jesus, who is for them. He also challenges them to see clearly that discipleship involves great risks and single-minded dedication.

STUDY QUESTION: Is the ethic of Christian discipleship really so rigidly either-or that it cannot tolerate an occasional both-and?

PERSECUTION BECAUSE OF PROPHETIC ATTACKS ON SHAM AND ABUSE OF POWER

37 He had just finished speaking when a Pharisee invited him to dine at his house. He went in and 38 sat down at the table. ·The Pharisee saw this and was surprised that he had not first washed before 39 the meal. ·But the Lord said to him, "Oh, you Pharisees! You clean the outside of cup and plate, while inside yourselves you are filled with ex-40 tortion and wickedness. ·Fools! Did not he who 41 made the outside make the inside too? ·Instead, give alms from what you have and then indeed 42 everything will be clean for you. ·But alas for you Pharisees! You who pay your tithe of mint and rue and all sorts of garden herbs and overlook justice and the love of God! These you should have practiced, without leaving the others undone.

43 Alas for you Pharisees who like taking the seats of honor in the synagogues and being greeted 44 obsequiously in the market squares! ·Alas for you, because you are like the unmarked tombs that men walk on without knowing it!

45 A lawyer then spoke up. "Master," he said, "when you speak like this you insult us too."

46 "Alas for you lawyers also," he replied, "because you load on men burdens that are unendurable, burdens that you yourselves do not move a finger to lift.

47 "Alas for you who build the tombs of the 48 prophets, the men your ancestors killed! ·In this way you both witness what your ancestors did and approve it; they did the killing, you do the building.

49   "And that is why the Wisdom of God said, 'I will send them prophets and apostles; some they
50 will slaughter and persecute, ·so that this generation will have to answer for every prophet's blood that has been shed since the foundation of the
51 world, ·from the blood of Abel to the blood of Zechariah, who was murdered between the altar and the sanctuary.' Yes, I tell you, this generation will have to answer for it all.

52   "Alas for you lawyers who have taken away the key of knowledge! You have not gone in yourselves, and have prevented others going in who wanted to."

53   When he left the house, the scribes and the Pharisees began a furious attack on him and tried to force answers from him on innumerable ques-
54 tions, ·setting traps to catch him out in something he might say.

✠

The sayings in this section are heavily paralleled in Matthew chapter 23 (see verses 4, 6, 7, 13, 23, 25, 27, 29–31, 34–36). Luke and Matthew have drawn these sayings from a common source. But neither Luke nor Matthew are much interested in preserving these historical records of Jesus the prophet's attacks on religious leaders of his day just for posterity's sake. For his part, Luke adapts these materials to buoy up his church, which faces opposition because it shares in Jesus' prophetic role. We can spy Luke's adaptations in verses 37, 41, and 49.

Luke sets this traditional material in the context of a meal with a Pharisee (11:37), a context he employs two other times to give teaching about the law (see 7:36 and 14:1). In 11:41 Luke touches upon one of his prominent themes, that of poor and rich, and gives the startling teaching that cleanliness before God is not achieved by external lustrations but by almsgiving. Proper participation at a meal in the Christian assembly is not governed by rules of handwashing but is open to the needy and those who have aided them (see 16: 19–31; Ac 2:41–47 and 4:31–35; contrast Lk 16:14).

Luke's hand is also tipped in 11:49, where he writes "prophets and apostles," which contrasts with Matthew's "prophets and wise men and scribes" (Mt 23:34). Like the prophets of old, Jesus the prophet (see 7:39, 24:19) did not shrink from condemning the sham and corrupt teaching of the powers-that-be. For his efforts, he suffered martyrdom. Christian prophets and apostles, commissioned by Jesus and sharing in his ministry, are experiencing similar treatment in Luke's day.

In the previous sections of this chapter (11:1–13, 11:14–36) we noted that Luke's purpose is to console and challenge his besieged church. In this section we glimpse one reason why his church may have been under fire. In attacking the abuse of power of their contemporary religious leaders, Luke's church cannot expect a more favorable reception than that accorded Jesus, their prophetic leader on the way.

STUDY QUESTIONS: Are prophetic attacks on governmental corruption and policy unpatriotic? Are prophetic challenges of ecclesiastical policy and law irreligious?

Luke 12:1–12
CONSOLATION FOR HARASSED CHRISTIANS

12 [1] Meanwhile the people had gathered in their thousands so that they were treading on one another. And he began to speak, first of all to his disciples. "Be on your guard against the yeast of [2] the Pharisees—that is, their hypocrisy. •Everything that is now covered will be uncovered, and every- [3] thing now hidden will be made clear. •For this reason, whatever you have said in the dark will be heard in the daylight, and what you have whispered in hidden places will be proclaimed on the housetops.

[4] "To you my friends I say: Do not be afraid of those who kill the body and after that can do no [5] more. •I will tell you whom to fear: fear him who, after he has killed, has the power to cast into hell. [6] Yes, I tell you, fear him. •Can you not buy five sparrows for two pennies? And yet not one is for- [7] gotten in God's sight. •Why, every hair on your head has been counted. There is no need to be afraid: you are worth more than hundreds of sparrows.

[8] "I tell you, if anyone openly declares himself for me in the presence of men, the Son of Man will declare himself for him in the presence of [9] God's angels. •But the man who disowns me in the presence of men will be disowned in the presence of God's angels.

[10] "Everyone who says a word against the Son of Man will be forgiven, but he who blasphemes against the Holy Spirit will not be forgiven.

[11] "When they take you before synagogues and magistrates and authorities, do not worry about

12 how to defend yourselves or what to say, ·because
when the time comes, the Holy Spirit will teach
you what you must say."

⊹

At first blush this section seems somewhat disjointed;
there is no underlying theme. Closer examination, however, will reveal that the section is unified around the
theme of consolation for Christians harassed because
they own up to their faith in Jesus.

The disciples, the Christians of Luke's day (12:1),
are warned that the Christian message cannot be hidden. Its nature demands that it be proclaimed from the
rooftops. It will not thrive in the security provided by
closed doors and smoke-filled rooms (12:3). And when
that message is proclaimed, its preachers are apt to encounter opposition. Their natural fear of such harass-
ment is assuaged as they realize that they are Jesus'
friends, precious in God's sight (12:4–7). Although
their fate may be death for avowing allegiance to Jesus,
they are further succored by the assurance that at the
judgment Jesus, the Son of Man, will intercede for those
who have fearlessly witnessed to him (12:8–9).

Luke 12:10 is a most perplexing verse which seems
to mean that those who have rejected Jesus, the Son
of Man, are forgiven. They are given a second chance
in the preaching of the Christian missionaries who are
equipped for their mission by the Holy Spirit (see Ac
1:8). There is no appeal from a second rejection.

Both Jewish and Gentile authorities harass the Christians, who are comforted by the fact that they have the
best defense attorney available, the Holy Spirit. See
Acts 4:8, where Peter "filled with the Holy Spirit,"
gives a sterling defense of his actions before the Jewish
authorities.

The Christians of Luke's day need the encouragement given to the Christians at Antioch: "We all have to experience many hardships before we enter the kingdom of God" (Ac 14:22).

STUDY QUESTION: A wag once remarked, "See how those Christians love to suffer." Is it possible to follow Jesus on his way without encountering opposition?

THE CHRISTIAN HEART,
TORN BETWEEN GOD AND POSSESSIONS

13   A man in the crowd said to him, "Master, tell my brother to give me a share of our inheritance."
14 "My friend," he replied, "who appointed me your
15 judge, or the arbitrator of your claims?" ·Then he said to them, "Watch, and be on your guard against avarice of any kind, for a man's life is not made secure by what he owns, even when he has more than he needs."
16   Then he told them a parable: "There was once a rich man who, having had a good harvest from
17 his hand, ·thought to himself, 'What am I to do?
18 I have not enough room to store my crops.' ·Then he said, 'This is what I will do: I will pull down my barns and build bigger ones, and store all my
19 grain and my goods in them, ·and I will say to my soul: My soul, you have plenty of good things laid by for many years to come; take things easy,
20 eat, drink, have a good time.' ·But God said to him, 'Fool! This very night the demand will be made for your soul; and this hoard of yours,
21 whose will it be then?' ·So it is when a man stores up treasure for himself in place of making himself rich in the sight of God."
22   Then he said to his disciples, "That is why I am telling you not to worry about your life and what you are to eat, nor about your body and how you
23 are to clothe it. ·For life means more than food,
24 and the body more than clothing. ·Think of the ravens. They do not sow or reap; they have no storehouses and no barns; yet God feeds them. And how much more are you worth than the
25 birds! ·Can any of you, for all his worrying, add

²⁶ a single cubit to his span of life? ·If the smallest
   things, therefore, are outside your control, why
²⁷ worry about the rest? ·Think of the flowers; they
   never have to spin or weave; yet, I assure you, not
   even Solomon in all his regalia was robed like one
²⁸ of these. ·Now if that is how God clothes the grass
   in the field which is there today and thrown into
   the furnace tomorrow, how much more will he
²⁹ look after you, you men of little faith! ·But you,
   you must not set your hearts on things to eat and
³⁰ things to drink; nor must you worry. ·It is the
   pagans of this world who set their hearts on all
   these things. Your Father well knows you need
³¹ them. ·No; set your hearts on his kingdom, and
   these other things will be given you as well.
³² "There is no need to be afraid, little flock, for
   it has pleased your Father to give you the
   kingdom.
³³ "Sell your possessions and give alms. Get yourselves purses that do not wear out, treasure that
   will not fail you, in heaven where no thief can
³⁴ reach it and no moth destroy it. ·For where your
   treasure is, there will your heart be also.

✠

While the Lukan community is pressured from the
outside by persecution, life-style problems agitate it
from within. In this section Luke uses Jesus' teachings
to answer one of these problems: Do possessions hin-
der Christians from following Jesus on his way?

Luke fashions a solution to this problem by using
verses 15, 21, 31–32, and 33–34 to interpret the traditional parable of verses 16–20. It would seem that the
rich man had found security for life in the abundance
of his possessions (12:15). Yet as the ending of the
parable teaches (12:20), his security procedures had
foolishly failed to take God into consideration. Luke
12:21 notes another major flaw in his security plans;

he had been so selfishly wrapped up in amassing possessions for himself that he had neglected mercy to the poor. He should have made himself rich by selling some of his possessions, giving them in alms to the poor, and thus amassing treasure in heaven (12:33). The heart follows its treasure like a magnet. If that treasure is God, the Christian heart bypasses other attractions until it rests in God. If the treasure is material possessions, then the heart will chase after the glitter and enjoyment of things which are subject to change without notice and will neglect the needy (12:33–34).

Luke responds further to the problem facing his community in verses 22–32, whose introductory "That is why I am telling you" (12:22) links it to the preceding verses 13–21. In the face of the most common human situation imaginable—people scurrying about after necessities (12:30)—Christians are exhorted to put their sole trust in God, who cares for them (12:31). Such advice is radical and comforting, comforting especially for persecuted Christians who may be deprived of the necessities of life. They should not read opposition as a sign that God has withdrawn from them and gone into serene hiding. They are his beloved "little flock" for whom he cares and to whom he has promised a share in his life (12:32).

Luke's answer to the propertied in his community is general. The propertied must never think that they merit the title Almighty because of their enormous possessions and power. Subject to their creator, they must avoid the conduct of the rich fool like cancer. Further, Christian possessors can never be relieved of their obligation to share their possessions with the poor. Luke stops short of teaching that wealth and its power are evil. Nor does he enjoin well-to-do Christians to sell *all* their possessions and give alms. But he does make it clear that the Christian heart must put its entire trust in God and not in possessions. Propertied Christians are challenged to draw their own conclusions (see Ac 2: 41–47, 4:31–35).

STUDY QUESTIONS: Is Luke's advice to Christian possessors wishy-washy? Is it possible to apply Luke's teaching in a society which honors capitalism and governmental welfare programs for the needy?

Luke 12:35–48
WATCHFULNESS MEANS
SELFLESS FIDELITY

35 "See that you are dressed for action and have
36 your lamps lit. ·Be like men waiting for their master to return from the wedding feast, ready to
open the door as soon as he comes and knocks.
37 Happy those servants whom the master finds
awake when he comes. I tell you solemnly, he
will put on an apron, sit them down at table
38 and wait on them. ·It may be in the second watch
he comes, or in the third, but happy those ser-
39 vants if he finds them ready. ·You may be quite
sure of this, that if the householder had known
at what hour the burglar would come, he would
not have let anyone break through the wall of
40 his house. ·You too must stand ready, because
the Son of Man is coming at an hour you do
not expect."
41 Peter said, "Lord, do you mean this parable for
42 us, or for everyone?" ·The Lord replied, "What
sort of steward, then, is faithful and wise enough
for the master to place him over his household to
give them their allowance of food at the proper
43 time? ·Happy that servant if his master's arrival
44 finds him at this employment. ·I tell you truly, he
45 will place him over everything he owns. ·But as for
the servant who says to himself, 'My master is
taking his time coming,' and sets about beating
the menservants and the maids, and eating and
46 drinking and getting drunk, ·his master will come
on a day he does not expect and at an hour he
does not know. The master will cut him off and
send him to the same fate as the unfaithful.
47 "The servant who knows what his master wants,

but has not even started to carry out those wishes,
⁴⁸ will receive very many strokes of the lash. ·The
one who did not know, but deserves to be beaten
for what he has done, will receive fewer strokes.
When a man has had a great deal given him, a
great deal will be demanded of him; when a man
has had a great deal given him on trust, even
more will be expected of him.

✠

Luke is not finished unpacking the import of the vitally important parable of the rich fool (12:16–20). In
this section he employs additional sayings of Jesus to
explicate 12:20: "But God said to him, 'Fool! This
very night the demand will be made for your soul; and
this hoard of yours, whose will it be then?'" The rich
fool was not ready for the coming of the Lord; Christians must be. Luke has a double position on when the
Lord comes. Here he portrays his coming at the individual's death, and not at the final judgment.

If servants go to bed at sundown, they must make
superior efforts to fight back sleep and be ready for
their master's return at midnight or later (12:35–38).
The master graces his watchful servants in an unbeliev-
able way. He hosts them to a meal and waits on them
himself. The Lord, who at the Last Supper calls himself a servant (22:27), rewards his faithful followers
in a most personal way.

In 12:41 Luke has Peter ask a question about the
parable of 12:35–38, and in the response (12:42)
changes the "servant" of the parable to "steward." By
these two modifications of the source he has in common
with Matthew (see Mt 24:43–51, especially 24:44–
45), Luke teaches that while readiness is an obligation
enjoined on all Christians, it weighs most heavily on

the church leaders, represented by Peter. They are the stewards of the church, the master's deputies in his absence. If they abuse their trust, maltreat church members, and squander the master's possessions in selfish living, their fate will be dire. Their conduct merits exclusion from the faithful and inclusion among the ranks of the nonbelievers (12:46). God has given many good gifts to them and will expect much of them (12:47–48). Church leaders are stewards and not members of some power elite who are entitled to regard God's manifold gifts as a free ticket to ignore him and to navel-gaze at their own importance (see further the rich fool's attitudes in 12:16–20).

STUDY QUESTION: If things are wrong with the church, are church leaders always to blame?

CONTINUED READINESS MEANS CONTINUAL REPENTANCE

49 "I have come to bring fire to the earth, and how
50 I wish it were blazing already! ·There is a baptism I must still receive, and how great is my distress till it is over!

51 "Do you suppose that I am here to bring peace
52 on earth? No, I tell you, but rather division. ·For from now on a household of five will be divided:
53 three against two and two against three; ·the father divided against the son, son against father, mother against daughter, daughter against mother, mother-in-law against daughter-in-law, daughter-in-law against mother-in-law."

54 He said again to the crowds, "When you see a cloud looming up in the west you say at once that
55 rain is coming, and so it does. ·And when the wind is from the south you say it will be hot, and it is.
56 Hypocrites! You know how to interpret the face of the earth and the sky. How is it you do not know how to interpret these times?

57 "Why not judge for yourselves what is right?
58 For example: when you go to court with your opponent, try to settle with him on the way, or he may drag you before the judge and the judge hand you over to the bailiff and the bailiff have you
59 thrown into prison. ·I tell you, you will not get out till you have paid the very last penny."

1 13 It was just about this time that some people arrived and told him about the Galileans whose blood Pilate had mingled with that of their
2 sacrifices. ·At this he said to them, "Do you suppose these Galileans who suffered like that were

3 greater sinners than any other Galileans? ·They
were not, I tell you. No; but unless you repent
4 you will all perish as they did. ·Or those eighteen
on whom the tower at Siloam fell and killed them?
Do you suppose that they were more guilty than
5 all the other people living in Jerusalem? ·They
were not, I tell you. No; but unless you repent
you will all perish as they did."
6   He told this parable: "A man had a fig tree
planted in his vineyard, and he came looking for
7 fruit on it but found none. ·He said to the man
who looked after the vineyard, 'Look here, for
three years now I have been coming to look for
fruit on this fig tree and finding none. Cut it
down: why should it be taking up the ground?'
8 'Sir,' the man replied, 'leave it one more year and
9 give me time to dig around it and manure it: ·it
may bear fruit next year; if not, then you can cut
it down.'"

✠

In this section Luke has garnered materials which detail the response people must give to Jesus, God's messenger. He utilizes these historical records to confront
his persecuted church once again with the message of
continual readiness for the Lord's return (see
12:35–48). He knows that the flip side of consolation
in trial is exhortation to steadfastness. After providing
brief comments on individual verses, we conclude with
a summary statement.

12:49–50 Jesus applies the judgment terms of fire and
water—fire and water purify—to himself. Jesus brings
the purifying fire of judgment in his preaching. Perhaps
Luke also thinks of the fire of the Holy Spirit which
Jesus sends (see Ac 2:3). Jesus' baptism is the purifica-
tion of his passion and death (see Mk 10:38–39).

12:54–59 The crowds are quite capable of reading indicators of rain and heat. But they will not lift a finger to evaluate Jesus' preaching (12:54–56). Luke challenges his church to regard the serious consequences of such noninvolvement (12:57–59).

13:1–9 Jesus rejects the common view that the quantity of one's sufferings evidences the amount of one's guilt (13:2, 4). The Galileans and the eighteen who perished in Jerusalem exemplify the necessity of continued repentance lest death find one unprepared. Perhaps the fig tree planted in the vineyard is Jerusalem (13:6–9; recall that in the Old Testament Israel is frequently likened to God's vineyard, e.g., Is 5:1–6). The ministry of Jesus and the church allowed additional time for Jerusalem to heed Jesus' message.

Luke 12:49 to 13:9 centers on the theme of the necessity of the church's persevering response to Jesus amidst persecution. Luke exhorts his fellow Christians not to become lackluster readers of the signs of the time. They must involve themselves in the consequences of continuing to follow Jesus. Repentance is not something which one does once and forgets (see 17:4, 9:23). It's like marriage vows, which are pronounced at one particular time but must be renewed daily if the marriage is not to crumble, especially in times of severe stress.

STUDY QUESTION: Luke's Gospel is hailed as the Gospel of God's mercy and love. Does this passage of threats belie that description?

THE CHURCH'S MISSION WILL SUCCEED

10 One sabbath day he was teaching in one of the
11 synagogues, •and a woman was there who for
eighteen years had been possessed by a spirit that
left her enfeebled; she was bent double and quite
12 unable to stand upright. •When Jesus saw her he
called her over and said, "Woman, you are rid of
13 your infirmity," •and he laid his hands on her.
And at once she straightened up, and she glorified
God.

14 But the synagogue official was indignant because Jesus had healed on the sabbath, and he
addressed the people present. "There are six
days," he said, "when work is to be done. Come
and be healed on one of those days and not on the
15 sabbath." •But the Lord answered him. "Hypocrites!" he said. "Is there one of you who does
not untie his ox or his donkey from the manger
16 on the sabbath and take it out for watering? •And
this woman, a daughter of Abraham whom Satan
has held bound these eighteen years—was it not
right to untie her bonds on the sabbath day?"
17 When he said this, all his adversaries were covered
with confusion, and all the people were overjoyed
at all the wonders he worked.

18 He went on to say, "What is the kingdom of
19 God like? What shall I compare it with? •It is like
a mustard seed which a man took and threw into
his garden: it grew and became a tree, and the
birds of the air sheltered in its branches."

20 Another thing he said, "What shall I compare
21 the kingdom of God with? •It is like the yeast a
woman took and mixed in with three measures of
flour till it was leavened all through."

✠

This section is a fitting conclusion to the first portion
of the travel narrative (9:51 to 13:21). By joining the
story of the healing of a daughter of Abraham (13:10–
17) to the twin parables of the mustard seed and yeast
(13:18–21), Luke has fashioned another message of
consolation for his persecuted community. We will
comment verse by verse on this rich material.

13:10 This is one of the few miracle stories Luke has
used in his travel narrative, which is almost ninety per
cent teaching material (see 14:1–6, 17:11–19, 18:35–
42; consult 11:14). The tag "miracle story," however,
should not blind us to the fact that these miracle stories
do not focus on Jesus' power, but are vehicles for teaching. The present miracle story is a case in point. Verses
14–17 recount Jesus' victory in a controversy about the
meaning of the sabbath.

13:11–13 The miracle is narrated with a modicum of
detail. Jesus is so concerned about the welfare of
human life that he takes no precautions against con-
tracting ritual impurity through contact with a woman—
a sick one at that. The woman praises God for what
God has done for her through Jesus.

13:14–16 The controversy commences. The synagogue official is incensed over the "violation" of the
sabbath and chides Jesus indirectly by admonishing the
people. He interprets Jesus' miracle not as a sign of
God's power at work in Jesus, but as mere work
(13:14). Jesus argues that if one can legitimately untie
an animal on the sabbath, he surely could untie this

woman's bonds. Only when God's creation has been liberated from the power of Satan (see 11:20), will Jesus rest on the sabbath. Until that time, it is right to heal on the sabbath. Thus, the synagogue official has erred in two regards. Jesus' ministry is not work, but God's attack against Satan's blight on creation. The sabbath law of rest does not prohibit care for someone in need.

13:17 This verse concludes both the miracle story and the controversy. Although suffering opposition, Jesus and the church will be successful in their mission of caring for the betterment of the human condition. God's reign will conquer the intrigues of men and Satan.

13:18–19 Since the parable of the mustard seed is joined directly to verse 17 by "He went on to say" (13:18), it furthers the message of success. Jesus' and the church's work for the establishment of God's kingdom is like the mustard seed. Proverbially the most insignificant of seeds, this seed attains the prominence of a tree. It may seem that Jesus' ministry and that of the church, small in scope and success, will amount to nothing. The parable warns against drawing this conclusion.

13:20–21 This twin of the first parable communicates the same message of success. Those of us who bake are amazed at the huge amount of flour the woman uses —some 190 cups. Despite its apparent insignificance, a little yeast affects every single particle of the bathtubful of flour. To be sure, Jesus' ministry and that of the church seem to be hardly worth a second glance. That is no reason for despair or inquietude.

Throughout this first portion of the travel narrative Luke has been concerned with a church undergoing persecution and has used Jesus' sayings to console and exhort his fellow Christians (see, e.g., 11:1–13, 12:1–12). This section develops the theme of consolation once more. What God has in mind for the ministry of Jesus and the church will come to pass. The church may seem trivial, but as in the case of the mustard seed and yeast first appearances are deceptive.

STUDY QUESTION: Luke does not provide timetables or growth charts for the parables of 13:18–21. How is it possible to know when the church is successful in its mission?

Luke 13:22–35
DON'T REST ON YOUR LAURELS

22 Through towns and villages he went teaching,
23 making his way to Jerusalem. ·Someone said to
him, "Sir, will there be only a few saved?" He
24 said to them, ·"Try your best to enter by the
narrow door, because, I tell you, many will try to
enter and will not succeed.

25 "Once the master of the house has got up and
locked the door, you may find yourself knocking
on the door, saying, 'Lord, open to us,' but he will
answer, 'I do not know where you come from.'
26 Then you will find yourself saying, 'We once ate
and drank in your company; you taught in our
27 streets,' ·but he will reply, 'I do not know where
you come from. Away from me, all you wicked
men!'

28 "Then there will be weeping and grinding of
teeth, when you see Abraham and Isaac and Jacob
and all the prophets in the kingdom of God, and
29 yourselves turned outside. ·And men from east
and west, from north and south, will come to take
their places at the feast in the kingdom of God.

30 "Yes, there are those now last who will be first,
and those now first who will be last."

31 Just at this time some Pharisees came up.
"Go away," they said. "Leave this place, because
32 Herod means to kill you." ·He replied, "You may
go and give that fox this message: Learn that today and tomorrow I cast out devils and on the
33 third day attain my end. ·But for today and tomorrow and the next day I must go on, since it
would not be right for a prophet to die outside
Jerusalem.

34 "Jerusalem, Jerusalem, **you** that kill the proph-

ets and stone those who are sent to you! How
often have I longed to gather your children, as a
hen gathers her brood under her wings, and you
³⁵ refused! ·So be it! Your house will be left to you.
Yes, I promise you, you shall not see me till the
time comes when you say:

> Blessings on him who comes in the name of
> the Lord!"

☩

In this section, which begins a new portion of the
travel narrative (13:22 to 17:10), Luke unites Jesus'
sayings around the theme of Jerusalem (13:22, 33,
34–35).

When Luke was penning his Gospel, Jesus had already met a prophet's fate in Jerusalem (13:33);
Jerusalem and its Temple had already been destroyed
(13:34–35; translated more literally, verse 35 begins,
"So be it! Your house is forsaken to you"). Christians
perceived Jerusalem's destruction as God's judgment on
people who did not try their very best to enter by the
narrow door (13:24), who noised it about that they
had connections with Jesus (13:25–27), and who
thought that they had been assured seats at the head
table in the heavenly banquet (13:28–29). The sure
bets for first place came in last (13:30). But the destruction of Jerusalem may not have been God's final
word. The last part of verse 35 seems to imply that
the Jews will convert at some future date.

Luke's primary concern in this section, however, is
not with regaling his community with reasons why Jerusalem failed to respond to Jesus. He uses the facts of
Jesus' unbending demand for repentance (13:23–30)
and of Jerusalem's failure to heed that demand as
means of admonishing his own community. Luke's in-

tention is spied especially in verse 23, where one single individual asks Jesus a question and Luke begins Jesus' answer with "He said to *them*." Also, the "you" of Jesus' answers in verses 24–29 is plural, not singular. Jesus is addressing the Christians of Luke's time. These Christians must not gloat over what happened to Jerusalem. Luke exhorts them not to rest on their laurels. The shoo-ins of the other group did not make the winner's circle. The same can happen to you.

STUDY QUESTION: It's so easy to puzzle smugly over the disbelief of the Jews, and in so doing to unconsciously feed our latent anti-Semitic feelings. What makes us think that the Jews were less open to Jesus than any other group of people, ourselves included?

TABLE FELLOWSHIP IN
THE CHRISTIAN COMMUNITY

¹ 14 Now on a sabbath day he had gone for a meal to the house of one of the leading ² Pharisees; and they watched him closely. ·There ³ in front of him was a man with dropsy, ·and Jesus addressed the lawyers and Pharisees. "Is it against the law," he asked, "to cure a man on the ⁴ sabbath, or not?" ·But they remained silent, so he took the man and cured him and sent him ⁵ away. ·Then he said to them, "Which of you here, if his son falls into a well, or his ox, will not pull him out on a sabbath day without hesitation?" ⁶ And to this they could find no answer.

⁷ He then told the guests a parable, because he had noticed how they picked the places of honor. ⁸ He said this, ·"When someone invites you to a wedding feast, do not take your seat in the place of honor. A more distinguished person than you ⁹ may have been invited, ·and the person who invited you both may come and say, 'Give up your place to this man.' And then, to your embarrassment, you would have to go and take the lowest ¹⁰ place. ·No; when you are a guest, make your way to the lowest place and sit there, so that, when your host comes, he may say, 'My friend, move up higher.' In that way, everyone with you at the ¹¹ table will see you honored. ·For everyone who exalts himself will be humbled, and the man who humbles himself will be exalted."

¹² Then he said to his host, "When you give a lunch or a dinner, do not ask your friends, brothers, relations or rich neighbors, for fear they repay your courtesy by inviting you in return.

13 No; when you have a party, invite the poor, the
14 crippled, the lame, the blind; ·that they cannot pay
you back means that you are fortunate, because
repayment will be made to you when the virtuous
rise again."

15   On hearing this, one of those gathered around
the table said to him, "Happy the man who will be
16 at the feast in the kingdom of God!" ·But he said
to him, "There was a man who gave a great banquet, and he invited a large number of people.
17 When the time for the banquet came, he sent his
servant to say to those who had been invited,
18 'Come along: everything is ready now.' ·But all
alike started to make excuses. The first said, 'I
have bought a piece of land and must go and see
19 it. Please accept my apologies.' ·Another said, 'I
have bought five yoke of oxen and am on my way
to try them out. Please accept my apologies.'
20 Yet another said, 'I have just got married and so
am unable to come.'
21   "The servant returned and reported this to his
master. Then the householder, in a rage, said to
his servant, 'Go out quickly into the streets and
alleys of the town and bring in here the poor, the
22 crippled, the blind and the lame.' ·'Sir,' said the
servant, 'your orders have been carried out and
23 there is still room.' ·Then the master said to his
servant, 'Go to the open roads and the hedgerows
and force people to come in to make sure my
24 house is full; ·because, I tell you, not one of those
who were invited shall have a taste of my
banquet.' "

✠

As you glance through this section, you will notice
that it consists of statements Jesus makes while taking
a meal with a leading Pharisee. In 14:1–6 the meal is
the setting for Jesus' interpretation of the sabbath law
of rest. Scrambling for the first places at table is the

subject of Jesus' remarks in verses 7-11. In verses 12-14 Jesus gives instructions on how to go about making up a guest list. Jesus tells the parable of the great banquet in verses 15-24. Luke has taken these sayings, spoken by Jesus on different occasions, and has unified them around a single meal setting. By composing the symposium of 14:1-24, Luke gives answers to a burning question within his church—who is worthy to share table fellowship? We highlight key points by moving through the section passage by passage. A statement of Luke's purpose concludes our commentary.

14:1-6 This story, very similar to that of 6:6-11, introduces the entire section and illustrates what Jesus has just said about his ministry in 13:32; he heals as well as casts out demons. The lawyers and the Pharisees are all eyes and seek to catch Jesus out in an error (14:1; see 11:53-54). Jesus gains the ascendancy in the implicit controversy about the meaning of the sabbath; care for the betterment of human life transcends the sabbath law of rest.

14:7-11 Not being a first-century Emily Post, Jesus does not teach a lesson in etiquette, but scores the religious leaders for using the occasion of table fellowship to seek plaudits for themselves. Such self-serving pride impairs table fellowship and does not impress God (14:11).

14:12-14 For this passage to make sense there must have been members of Luke's church who had the wherewithal to host festive meals. Jesus' instructions on how to make out the invitation list for such meals is revolutionary, especially for Luke's readers, who come from a culture which endorses an ethic of reciprocity:

Put your friends in your debt, so that at some future time you can cash in on their IOUs. These readers are admonished to work up a new invitation list which includes the social and religious outcasts of the day (the crippled, the lame, and the blind were excluded from Temple worship because of their ills). These undesirables cannot repay their hosts. God will do that.

14:15–24 When one of those at the table piously notes that those (himself included?) who get to feast at the heavenly banquet will truly be happy, he provides an opening for Jesus' final teaching. There are two major points to the parable of the snubbed invitation. One is the excuses which the invited folk give in verses 18–20. It seems rather incongruous that they would have waited until suppertime to inspect land, try oxen, and set up a new household. Their excuses are lame; they are just too caught up in earthly concerns to heed the invitation. These excuses are typical of the ones which people give in Luke's own day. The second major point is that verse 22 repeats verse 13; the poor, the crippled, the blind, and the lame. Those who would seem to be excluded from the banquet because of their social or cultic liabilities actually grace the banquet tables. The ones who refused to come, even if they change their minds, will not taste a single succulent morsel of the banquet. The house is full (14:23).

Luke explores Jesus' rich image of table fellowship to admonish the prosperous and smug of his community. These are the ones who have an inflated view of themselves and who abuse church celebrations to polish their image (14:7–11). They are tempted to avoid the "undesirables" of the community (14:12–14). They immerse themselves in the cares of this world and yawn in the face of Jesus' invitation to repent and share genuine table fellowship with him. Despite the protestations of the powerful, Jesus does not exclude the poor, the crippled, the lame, and the blind from table fellowship with God, nor does his church (see 15:1–2).

STUDY QUESTIONS: How open are churches to today's undesirables? Do church members and leaders succumb to the temptation of using table fellowship as a steppingstone to self-importance?

Luke 14:25–35
YOUR YES TO JESUS MUST
BE STEADFAST

25 Great crowds accompanied him on his way and
26 he turned and spoke to them. ·"If any man comes
to me without hating his father, mother, wife,
children, brothers, sisters, yes and his own life
27 too, he cannot be my disciple. ·Anyone who does
not carry his cross and come after me cannot be
my disciple.
28 "And indeed, which of you here, intending to
build a tower, would not first sit down and work
out the cost to see if he had enough to complete
29 it? ·Otherwise, if he laid the foundation and then
found himself unable to finish the work, the on-
lookers would all start making fun of him and
30 saying, ·'Here is a man who started to build and
31 was unable to finish.' ·Or again, what king march-
ing to war against another king would not first sit
down and consider whether with ten thousand
men he could stand up to the other who advanced
32 against him with twenty thousand? ·If not, then
while the other king was still a long way off, he
33 would send envoys to sue for peace. ·So in the
same way, none of you can be my disciple unless
he gives up all his possessions.
34 "Salt is a useful thing. But if the salt itself loses
35 its taste, how can it be seasoned again? ·It is good
for neither soil nor manure heap. People throw it
out. Listen, anyone who has ears to hear!"

✠

In this section Luke gathers sayings of Jesus to exhort his church to steadfast discipleship. After com-

menting on individual passages, we single out Luke's theme of poor and rich for further discussion.

14:25 The "great crowds" which accompany Jesus represent the multitudes who will join the Christian community (see the thousands mentioned in Acts 2:41 and 4:4).

14:26–27 The "hating" of 14:26 is a Semitic way of expressing total detachment. To be a steadfast disciple demands much, especially when the prospects of persecution at home and from authorities are so awesome.

14:28–32 These twin parables are sandwiched between the first two discipleship sayings (14:26–27) and the final one (14:33). The point of the parables is sage planning. Weigh the costs before you embark on a project. Otherwise, you will not be able to complete it and will become the butt of countless jokes.

14:33 This verse must be interpreted in context. Verses 26–27, where the first two "cannot be my disciple" statements occur, suggests a persecution context also for verse 33. This verse builds upon the twin parables of verses 28–32 by highlighting the shame and disgrace of the person who starts something which he is not able to finish. Thus, the context indicates that verse 33 does not lay down the unconditional demand that people must sell all their possessions before they can become disciples of Jesus. Rather, it has in view Christian disciples who would allow their possessions to put a halt to their continued walk with Jesus. The situation behind verse 33 may be reflected in another part of the New Testament: "For you not only shared in the sufferings of those who were in prison, but you happily accepted being stripped of your belongings, knowing that you owned something that was better and lasting" (Heb 10:34). Viewed in its context, 14:33 could be paraphrased, "If it's a choice between me and your possessions, you must show your love for me by abandoning all your possessions."

14:34–35 The saying about salt describes the fate of the disciple who denies Jesus during persecution.

Luke 14:33 is one of the most important building blocks in Luke's theme of poor and rich. It cannot be dismissed out of hand with the casual remark that it's just another instance of Semitic hyperbole like verse 26. Discipleship is serious business, especially for those who have possessions. Luke advises his prosperous community that the cost of discipleship has skyrocketed because of persecution. If they want to live as disciples, then they have to pay the price.

STUDY QUESTION: Jesus, like any lover, demands much. Are his demands in this section unreasonable?

Luke 15:1–32
OPEN YOUR HEARTS AND
IMITATE GOD'S MERCY

^{1} $\mathbf{15}$ The tax collectors and the sinners, mean-while, were all seeking his company to hear ^{2} what he had to say, ·and the Pharisees and the scribes complained. "This man," they said, "wel- ^{3} comes sinners and eats with them." ·So he spoke this parable to them:

^{4} "What man among you with a hundred sheep, losing one, would not leave the ninety-nine in the wilderness and go after the missing one till he ^{5} found it? ·And when he found it, would he not ^{6} joyfully take it on his shoulders ·and then, when he got home, call together his friends and neigh-bors? 'Rejoice with me,' he would say, 'I have ^{7} found my sheep that was lost.' ·In the same way, I tell you, there will be more rejoicing in heaven over one repentant sinner than over ninety-nine virtuous men who have no need of repentance.

^{8} "Or again, what woman with ten drachmas would not, if she lost one, light a lamp and sweep out the house and search thoroughly till she found ^{9} it? ·And then, when she had found it, call together her friends and neighbors? 'Rejoice with me,' she ^{10} would say, 'I have found the drachma I lost.' ·In the same way, I tell you, there is rejoicing among the angels of God over one repentant sinner."

$^{11}_{12}$ He also said, "A man had two sons. ·The younger said to his father, 'Father, let me have the share of the estate that would come to me.' So the ^{13} father divided the property between them. ·A few days later, the younger son got together every-thing he had and left for a distant country where he squandered his money on a life of debauchery.

14   "When he had spent it all, that country experienced a severe famine, and now he began to feel
15   the pinch, ·so he hired himself out to one of the
local inhabitants who put him on his farm to feed
16   the pigs. ·And he would willingly have filled his
belly with the husks the pigs were eating but no
17   one offered him anything. ·Then he came to his
senses and said, 'How many of my father's paid
servants have more food than they want, and here
18   am I dying of hunger! ·I will leave this place and
go to my father and say: Father, I have sinned
19   against heaven and against you; ·I no longer de-
serve to be called your son; treat me as one of
20   your paid servants.' ·So he left the place and went
back to his father.

"While he was still a long way off, his father
saw him and was moved with pity. He ran to the
boy, clasped him in his arms and kissed him ten-
21   derly. ·Then his son said, 'Father, I have sinned
against heaven and against you. I no longer de-
22   serve to be called your son.' ·But the father said to
his servants, 'Quick! Bring out the best robe and
put it on him; put a ring on his finger and sandals
23   on his feet. ·Bring the calf we have been fattening,
and kill it; we are going to have a feast, a cele-
24   bration, ·because this son of mine was dead and
has come back to life; he was lost and is found.'
And they began to celebrate.

25   "Now the elder son was out in the fields, and on
his way back, as he drew near the house, he could
26   hear music and dancing. ·Calling one of the
27   servants he asked what it was all about. ·'Your
brother has come,' replied the servant, 'and your
father has killed the calf we had fattened because
28   he has got him back safe and sound.' ·He was
angry then and refused to go in, and his father
29   came out to plead with him; ·but he answered his
father, 'Look, all these years I have slaved for you
and never once disobeyed your orders, yet you
never offered me so much as a kid for me to cele-
30   brate with my friends. ·But, for this son of yours,
when he comes back after swallowing up your

property—he and his women—you kill the calf we had been fattening.'

31   "The father said, 'My son, you are with me
32 always and all I have is yours. ·But it was only right we should celebrate and rejoice, because your brother here was dead and has come to life; he was lost and is found.' "

✠

The parable of the Prodigal Son has topped the best-seller lists for centuries. Virtually everyone is familiar with this masterpiece. What follows is a quest for a richer understanding of this most familiar masterpiece. We begin with specific remarks on important verses in chapter 15 and conclude with a panoramic view of the parable in the entire context of the chapter.

GENERAL REMARKS

15:4   This verse spotlights the apparent recklessness of the shepherd who leaves ninety-nine sheep untended to care for the single lost sheep.

15:7   Does God really care for the ninety-nine just? He seems to be all bent on caring for the one lost one. An analogy provides an answer: When parents lavish more love on their sick child, that doesn't mean that they love their other children less.

15:8–10   It is revolutionary that a woman, a member of an "outcast" class in antiquity, provides an image of God's activity in Jesus. A rule of thumb may help us get a handle on the troublesome "drachma" and therefore on the meaning of this parable. This silver coin, worth a day's wages, should not be visualized by weight, like a dime, but by purchasing power. None but a miser would scour the house for a dime, but most would turn the place upside down to find the equivalent of a day's wages.

15:13 "Where he squandered his money on a life of debauchery." This translation is too sensuous. The meaning of the Greek is, "The younger son squandered his money by being a spendthrift." Colloquially, he blew his inheritance. It is only in verse 30 that the older son claims that his brother dissipated his money on whores. This is an obvious slur and does not provide unbiased evidence for the kind of sin the younger son committed.

15:17, 19 "Treat me as one of your paid servants." The younger son has a mistaken view of himself and his father. He really is his father's son and not a paid servant. The father's forgiveness prompts the younger son to throw off the category of the mercenary and to put on the consciousness of being loved as a son.

15:18, 21 "I have sinned against heaven and against you." What was the younger son's sin? He had dissipated his means of caring for his father in case a necessity, like incapacitating illness, arose.

15:20 "He ran to the boy." The father's conduct is extraordinary and somewhat undignified. One would not expect an elderly oriental father to catch up his garments and run.

15:22 "Bring out the best robe and put it on him; put a ring on his finger and sandals on his feet." The father's forgiveness is acted out. The prodigal is not a paid servant, but wears the trappings of an honored son.

15:29 "I have slaved for you." Behind the seemingly innocuous "I have slaved" lies a misunderstanding. Like his younger brother, the older brother has a mistaken, mercenary view of the man who is his *father*. The younger lad is not a "paid servant" of his father nor is the older lad a "slave" of his father. Both are *sons*. Unless the older lad grasps this fact, he cannot treat the younger lad as his brother. The father's forgiveness is meant to shatter the mercenary outlook of his two sons. The younger son accepts that forgiveness. The parable is open-ended and does not tell us whether the elder son accepted his father as forgiving father and his brother as forgiven brother.

15:30–32 These verses continue the point of verse 29. The elder son retorts to his father, "But, for this son of yours." The father addresses his elder son as "my son" and refers to the younger lad as "your brother."

These general remarks have put us on the threshold of a richer understanding of the parable of the Prodigal Son. They have also hinted that this parable cannot be considered in isolation from the rest of the chapter. Let us take a panoramic view of the vista which Luke has created by linking this parable with the rest of chapter 15.

THE PARABLE OF THE PRODIGAL SON IN ITS CONTEXT

Since Luke is no curator of museum pieces which he merely dusts off before presenting them to his gen-

eration of Christians, we would expect him to hand on
the parable of the Prodigal Son in a creatively new way.
He does not disappoint our expectations. One feature
of Luke's creativity is to combine three, once independent parables into this unit of teaching. Apparently he
had prior help as the traditional refrain of "rejoice, lost,
found" in verses 6, 9, 24, and 32 intimates:

> "*Rejoice* with me," he would say, "I have *found*
> my sheep that was lost" (15:6).
>
> "*Rejoice* with me," she would say, "I have
> *found* the drachma I lost" (15:9).
>
> "We are going to have a feast, a *celebration,*
> because this son of mine was dead and has
> come back to life; he was *lost* and is *found*"
> (15:23–24).
>
> "But it was only right we should celebrate and
> *rejoice,* because your brother here was dead and
> has come to life; he was *lost* and is *found*"
> (15:32).

This refrain clearly links the three parables together.

While Luke retained this merely literary way of linking the three parables, he added two more substantive
connections of his own. First, it is Luke who is responsible for verses 7 and 10, which feature repentant sinners, a prize Lukan theme. Thus, Luke has transformed
the meaning of "lost and found" in the first two parables to accord with the meaning of "lost and found"
in the third parable. No longer is the object of the
search something impersonal—a sheep or coin. Now it
is human, and all three parables deal with God's search
for the human sinner who repents. Secondly, Luke in-

troduces the three closely connected parables by means
of verses 1 and 2 (see 5:30). Thus, Luke does not
allow the three parables to float about anchorless, but
addresses them to the complaining Pharisees—people of
his own time. This motif of complaining, absent from
the twin parables of lost sheep and lost coin, resurfaces
in verses 28–30 as the elder son voices his angry dis-
approval of his father's action. By the motif of complaining, Luke has joined the beginning and the end of
the chapter together.

Luke's extensive creativity in this chapter results in
a message which is beguilingly simple. Jesus' life is the
supreme revelation of God's relentlessly merciful love
for the repentant sinner, who may think of himself as
no more than a "paid servant" but in the act of forgiveness experiences God as father and himself as son.
Luke, however, does not hand on this message in a
vacuum. As our analysis of 15:1–2 has shown, he confronts the Pharisees of his church with it. These Pharisees are church members who sport a holier-than-thou
attitude and complain of repentant apostates and of the
"riffraff" they see streaming into the church. These
rigorists must cease viewing relationships with God in
tit-for-tat terms and must open their hearts to imitate
God's merciful sentiments toward sinners. Unless they
do that, they will fail to recognize God as merciful
father and the forgiven riffraff as their brothers and
sisters.

In sum, the members of Luke's church who lobby
for severe entrance requirements for sinners are confronted with the threefold tradition of Jesus, revealer
of the merciful Father. Their mercenary attitude of
"Give them and us our due" must give way to Jesus'
attitude of mercy.

STUDY QUESTIONS: How does the image of God presented in this chapter compare with a commonly held image of God, the heavenly accountant, poised to pounce on the slightest mistake? Are there any rigorists in the contemporary church? Does Jesus' teaching of God's mercy give a blank check to imitate the prodigal son?

THE POOR ARE MOST WORTHY
OF YOUR CONCERN

1 **16** He also said to his disciples, "There was a rich man and he had a steward who was denounced to him for being wasteful with his
2 property. ·He called for the man and said, 'What is this I hear about you? Draw me up an account of your stewardship because you are not to be my
3 steward any longer.' ·Then the steward said to himself, 'Now that my master is taking the stewardship from me, what am I to do? Dig? I am not strong enough. Go begging? I should be too
4 ashamed. ·Ah, I know what I will do to make sure that when I am dismissed from office there will be some to welcome me into their homes.'

5   "Then he called his master's debtors one by one. To the first he said, 'How much do you owe
6 my master?' ·'One hundred measures of oil,' was the reply. The steward said, 'Here, take your
7 bond; sit down straightaway and write fifty.' ·To another he said, 'And you, sir, how much do you owe?' 'One hundred measures of wheat,' was the reply. The steward said, 'Here, take your bond and write eighty.'

8   "The master praised the dishonest steward for his astuteness. For the children of this world are more astute in dealing with their own kind than are the children of light."

9   "And so I tell you this: use money, tainted as it is, to win you friends, and thus make sure that when it fails you, they will welcome you into the
10 tents of eternity. ·The man who can be trusted in little things can be trusted in great; the man who is dishonest in little things will be dishonest in

11 great. ·If then you cannot be trusted with money,
that tainted thing, who will trust you with genuine
12 riches? ·And if you cannot be trusted with what is
not yours, who will give you what is your very
own?

13   "No servant can be the slave of two masters: he
will either hate the first and love the second, or
treat the first with respect and the second with
scorn. You cannot be the slave both of God and
of money."

14   The Pharisees, who loved money, heard all this
15 and laughed at him. ·He said to them, "You are
the very ones who pass yourselves off as virtuous
in people's sight, but God knows your hearts. For
what is thought highly of by men is loathsome in
the sight of God.

16   "Up to the time of John it was the Law and the
Prophets; since then, the kingdom of God has
been preached, and by violence everyone is
getting in.

17   "It is easier for heaven and earth to disappear
than for one little stroke to drop out of the Law.

18   "Everyone who divorces his wife and marries
another is guilty of adultery, and the man who
marries a woman divorced by her husband commits adultery.

19   "There was a rich man who used to dress in
purple and fine linen and feast magnificently every
20 day. ·And at his gate there lay a poor man called
21 Lazarus, covered with sores, ·who longed to fill
himself with the scraps that fell from the rich
man's table. Dogs even came and licked his sores.
22 Now the poor man died and was carried away
by the angels to the bosom of Abraham. The
rich man also died and was buried.

23   "In his torment in Hades he looked up and saw
Abraham a long way off with Lazarus in his
24 bosom. ·So he cried out, 'Father Abraham, pity
me and send Lazarus to dip the tip of his finger in
water and cool my tongue, for I am in agony in
25 these flames.' ·'My son,' Abraham replied, 'remember that during your life good things came

your way, just as bad things came the way of
Lazarus. Now he is being comforted here while
26 you are in agony. ·But that is not all: between us
and you a great gulf has been fixed, to stop anyone, if he wanted to, crossing from our side to
yours, and to stop any crossing from your side to
ours.'
27   "The rich man replied, 'Father, I beg you then
28 to send Lazarus to my father's house, ·since I
have five brothers, to give them warning so that
they do not come to this place of torment too.'
29 'They have Moses and the prophets,' said Abra-
30 ham, 'let them listen to them.' ·'Ah no, father
Abraham,' said the rich man, 'but if someone
comes to them from the dead, they will repent.'
31 Then Abraham said to him, 'If they will not listen
either to Moses or to the prophets, they will not
be convinced even if someone should rise from the
dead.' "

☩

A popular view is that Jesus champions dishonesty
in the parable of the dishonest steward (16:1–13), and
this shocks people. Their shock is intensified these days
when white-collar crime gallops out of sight and Water-
gate is still an open wound. I recall the comment I recently received after preaching a well-nuanced sermon
on this parable, "Nice try, Father, but I still think that
Jesus shouldn't have praised dishonesty!" In our commentary on this section we will set the hornets' nest
of verses 1–13 within the larger context of all of chapter
16. Within this context we will be able to savor its true
meaning and to see how much it contributes to the
development of Luke's theme of poor and rich. We divide our comments into two parts, verses 1–13 and
verses 14–31.

16:1–13 Countless thousands have had difficulty getting a handle on the understanding of this passage because the economic situation behind the parable is foreign to our culture. The steward was empowered to make legally binding bonds or contracts for his master and was allowed by the customs of the time to make a profit for himself on the deals he made. For example, John Jones would come and ask for a loan of eighty measures of wheat. He would get the eighty measures of wheat, but his bond or contract would be written up to read one hundred. The extra twenty measures of wheat were the steward's legitimate profit. When the very shrewd steward realized that he was going to get a pink slip because of his wastefulness, he moved quickly to forego his profits and issued new bonds. The beneficiaries of his alert thinking would surely welcome him into their homes after his dismissal. On the basis of this economic background it is plain that the master was not cheated out of anything due him and that the enterprising steward escaped the ordeals of digging and the shame of begging.

Simply put, the point of the parable is that the steward used his money astutely. Stated negatively, the parable does not teach that the master praised his steward because of his dishonesty. The conclusion to the parable is very clear, "The master praised the dishonest steward *for his astuteness*" (16:8a).

Luke uses the Jesus sayings in verses 8b–13 to apply the message of the parable to his own community. Are they as astute in money matters as the steward (16:8b)? They must use their money to give alms and gain the poor as their friends. When the money of those who gave alms runs out at death, they will gain access to heaven (16:9). Christians must remember that money is on loan from God. If they do not use this

little loan trustworthily, they will not be trusted with
that which really counts—eternal life (16:10–12).
Money may not be evil, but it can turn into a god which
controls every aspect of one's life. It is very difficult
to tightrope the issue of God and money. It's one or
the other (16:13). In sum, in verses 8b–13 Luke
makes the application of the parable of the prudent
steward quite specific for his fellow Christians—use your
possessions astutely by caring for the poor.

16:14–31 The Pharisees scoff at Jesus' teaching about
the use of possessions (16:14). These Pharisees are not
the ones whom Jesus encountered during his ministry,
but some people in Luke's own community who think
that Jesus' message about poor and rich is nonsense.
They seem to think that their possessions are a sure
sign of God's favor. Since that is the case, why should
they give them up for the despicable poor whose very
poverty shows in what low regard God holds them?
Jesus condemns the pride of these people who think
they have a corner of God's favor (16:15).

On the first reading, the one-liners of verses 16–18
do not seem to have anything to do with the theme of
poor and rich being developed in this chapter. There
are some connections, however. We have already seen
that in verse 15 Jesus rejected the view that wealth is
a sign of God's favor. The rich are not privileged in
God's sight; nor are others—not even the poor—excluded from God's kingdom (see the "everyone" of
16:16). Jesus has not abolished the Law and the
prophets and their teaching about almsgiving (16:17;
see the similar phrase, "Moses and the prophets," in
16:29 and 31). Thus, verses 16–17 add pointedly to
Luke's theme of poor and rich, for they show that Jesus

did not declare almsgiving a nonissue for the rich and powerful.

The first part (16:19–26) of the parable of the rich man and Lazarus does not explore the religious motivations of the two characters. Nor does it say that the rich man was coldhearted toward Lazarus, or that Lazarus was the epitome of patience. It is stated simply and plainly that their situations were reversed after death. Lazarus enjoys fellowship with Abraham, whereas the rich man is tormented. In verses 27–31 the parable takes on considerable religious coloring. It dawns on the rich man that his conduct toward Lazarus was wrong. He earnestly pleads for help so that his five brothers may repent of similar conduct before it is too late. Abraham reminds the rich man that his brothers have Moses and the prophets, whose teaching on care for the poor is still valid (see 16:17). Let them heed their teaching. If these are shrugged off as nonimportant, even the teachings of the risen Lord (16:31) will have no impact.

The largely negative teachings of verses 19–31 can be profitably contrasted with the positive instructions of verses 1–13. Verse 9 spotlights the conduct of a rich man who is attentive to the teachings of Moses and the prophets and gives alms to the poor. He is astute; his sight is directed on eternal life. By contrast, the rich man of verses 19–31 is distracted by the pleasures of this life and neglects to make Lazarus his friend by giving him alms. He needs a radical conversion, because money is the be-all and end-all of his life (16:13).

In chapter 16 Luke adds masterful strokes to his theme of poor and rich and presents a startling message for the possessors of his community. They must realize that their possessions are on loan from God and have to be used to benefit the poor. Anyone who thinks that his possessions are God's unconditional stamp of approval on his person and conduct has his theological head screwed on wrong. Wealth does not grant privileges; it's for the poor.

STUDY QUESTION: Religious movements in Third World countries have challenged us members of God's most favored nation to read the parable of the rich man and Lazarus anew. Are the poor in our country and abroad poor because of oppression and exploitation by the rich?

Luke 17:1–10
THE POWER AND NECESSITY OF FAITH

1 **17** He said to his disciples, "Obstacles are sure to come, but alas for the one who provides 2 them! ·It would be better for him to be thrown into the sea with a millstone put around his neck than that he should lead astray a single one of 3 these little ones. ·Watch yourselves!

"If your brother does something wrong, re-
4 prove him and, if he is sorry, forgive him. ·And if he wrongs you seven times a day and seven times comes back to you and says, 'I am sorry,' you must forgive him."

5 The apostles said to the Lord, "Increase our 6 faith." ·The Lord replied, "Were your faith the size of a mustard seed you could say to this mulberry tree, 'Be uprooted and planted in the sea,' and it would obey you.

7 "Which of you, with a servant plowing or minding sheep, would say to him when he re-turned from the fields, 'Come and have your meal 8 immediately?' ·Would he not be more likely to say, 'Get my supper laid; make yourself tidy and wait on me while I eat and drink. You can eat and 9 drink yourself afterward?' ·Must he be grateful to 10 the servant for doing what he was told? ·So with you: when you have done all you have been told to do, say, 'We are merely servants: we have done no more than our duty.'"

✠

In this section Luke uses Jesus' teaching about the power of faith (17:5–6) as the centerpiece around

which he clusters sayings of Jesus. These sayings sum-
marize lessons taught during the second portion of the
travel narrative (13:22 to 17:10)—care for the poor,
forgiveness, and perseverance during persecution.

It is inevitable that Christians will encounter temptations against faith, even from their fellow believers
(17:1–2). Woe to those who, like the rich man of
16:19–31, generate temptations for Christians like
Lazarus, "one of these little ones" (17:2).

Christians must ceaselessly share with one another
the forgiveness they receive (17:3–4; the symbolic
number "seven" means an unlimited number of times).
The Christian is not restricted to a single, once-for-all-
time "I am sorry, I repent." His fellow Christians must
accept his repeated "I am sorry." Recall the message
of chapter 15, "Imitate God's mercy."

The "apostles," who represent church leaders of
Luke's day, are fully aware of the difficulty created by
Jesus' demand to forgive ceaselessly and implore him,
"Increase our faith!" (17:5–6). Faith accomplishes the
impossible mission of repeated forgiveness.

Church leaders, who labor in missionary fields and
shepherd the local church, cannot expect special privileges (17:7–10). They may have successfully bucked
the most powerful waves of persecution, but this does
not entitle them to preferential treatment. They are
merely servants who must obey their master (remember
that the Apostle Paul often refers to himself as the "servant" of Jesus Christ, e.g., Rm 1:1). Since church leaders play in the superbowl of self-denial, faith is the only
thing that will see them through to victory.

In order to resist the seduction of wealth, to imitate
its forgiving Father, and to withstand the attacks of persecution, the Christian community prays to its Lord,
"Increase our faith!"

STUDY QUESTION: The contemporary phenomenon of faith healing has reawakened Christian churches to the power of faith in Jesus. Why have many Christian churches neglected this dimension of faith in Jesus?

Luke 17:11–19
SALVATION THROUGH FAITH
AND NOT THROUGH THE MIRACULOUS

11 Now on the way to Jerusalem he traveled along
12 the border between Samaria and Galilee. ·As he
   entered one of the villages, ten lepers came to
13 meet him. They stood some way off ·and called
14 to him, "Jesus! Master! Take pity on us." ·When
   he saw them he said, "Go and show yourselves to
   the priests." Now as they were going away they
15 were cleansed. ·Finding himself cured, one of
   them turned back praising God at the top of his
16 voice ·and threw himself at the feet of Jesus and
17 thanked him. The man was a Samaritan. ·This
   made Jesus say, "Were not all ten made clean?
18 The other nine, where are they? ·It seems that no
   one has come back to give praise to God, except
19 this foreigner." ·And he said to the man, "Stand
   up and go on your way. Your faith has saved
   you."

✠

This section opens the final portion of Luke's travel
narrative (17:11 to 19:44). As is true of the other
healings in the travel narrative (see 13:10–17, 14:1–6,
18:35–43), the focus of this story is not on the healing
as such (17:11–14) but on Jesus' teaching (17:15–
19). This observation is confirmed by the view pop-
ularized in sermons that the gist of the story is gratitude, a point first made in the teaching part of the story.

In verses 11–14 Jesus' power to cure—at a distance
—is in the forefront, and one is reminded of Jesus'

words to the two disciples of John the Baptist: "Go back and tell John what you have seen and heard: the blind see again, the lame walk, *lepers are cleansed* . . ." (7:22). Jesus is indeed "the one who is to come" (7:20).

Jesus' teaching dominates 17:15–19. The key words are: praise God (17:15, 18); a Samaritan, this foreigner (17:16, 18); your faith has saved you (17:19). The leper's return shows that he has grasped what Jesus' cure implies: God is operative in Jesus and must be praised. The mere experience of the cure did not save. By returning and praising God, the leper gives voice to the faith which saves him. "A Samaritan," "this foreigner" underline the unexpected, the startling. If anyone would be expected to return to Jesus to give thanks, it would be a Jew, not a despised Samaritan. The twofold emphasis given to the ethnic background of the grateful leper directs the reader's attention to the success of the Christian mission among the Samaritans (see Ac 8:1–25).

On one level the message of this section is gratitude. On a deeper level, however, Luke takes great pains to remind his fellow believers of the nature of salvation. When persecution is most intense, they might yearn for Jesus' miraculous intervention. But the experience of the miraculous is not salvation. Salvation is effected by their continued profession of praise and faith in the Jesus through whom God acts.

STUDY QUESTION: To what extent does this section suggest an answer to the oft-heard question, "If God is all powerful and loves me, why doesn't he save me from this suffering?"

20 Asked by the Pharisees when the kingdom of God was to come, he gave them this answer, "The coming of the kingdom of God does not admit 21 of observation ·and there will be no one to say, 'Look here! Look there!' For, you must know, the kingdom of God is among you."

22 He said to the disciples, "A time will come when you will long to see one of the days of the Son of 23 Man and will not see it. ·They will say to you, 'Look there!' or, 'Look here!' Make no move; do 24 not set off in pursuit; ·for as the lightning flashing from one part of heaven lights up the other, so will be the Son of Man when his day comes. 25 But first he must suffer grievously and be rejected by this generation.

26 "As it was in Noah's day, so will it also be in 27 the days of the Son of Man. ·People were eating and drinking, marrying wives and husbands, right up to the day Noah went into the ark, and the 28 Flood came and destroyed them all. ·It will be the same as it was in Lot's day: people were eating and drinking, buying and selling, planting and 29 building, ·but the day Lot left Sodom, God rained fire and brimstone from heaven and it destroyed 30 them all. ·It will be the same when the day comes for the Son of Man to be revealed.

31 "When that day comes, anyone on the house-top, with his possessions in the house, must not come down to collect them, nor must anyone in 32 the fields turn back either. ·Remember Lot's wife. 33 Anyone who tries to preserve his life will lose it; 34 and anyone who loses it will keep it safe. ·I tell you, on that night two will be in one bed: one

35 will be taken, the other left; ·two women will be grinding corn together: one will be taken, the
37 other left." ·The disciples interrupted. "Where, Lord?" they asked. He said, "Where the body is, there too will the vultures gather."

1 **18** Then he told them a parable about the need to pray continually and never lose heart.
2 "There was a judge in a certain town," he said, "who had neither fear of God nor respect for
3 man. ·In the same town there was a widow who kept on coming to him and saying, 'I want justice
4 from you against my enemy!' ·For a long time he refused, but at last he said to himself, 'Maybe I have neither fear of God nor respect for man,
5 but since she keeps pestering me I must give this widow her just rights, or she will persist in coming and worry me to death.' "
6 And the Lord said, "You notice what the unjust
7 judge has to say? ·Now will not God see justice done to his chosen who cry to him day and night
8 even when he delays to help them? ·I promise you, he will see justice done to them, and done speedily. But when the Son of Man comes, will he find any faith on earth?"

✠

Jesus taught that salvation is present in his teaching and deeds; he also taught that salvation has a future dimension. In this section Luke uses sayings of Jesus to solve problems which that future dimension created for his church, e.g., when will Jesus return in judgment? We comment on this section seriatim.

17:20–21 The coming of God's reign is not like the rising of stars which is susceptible to astrologer's observations and plottings. Nor can one track it and yell, "I've found it!" If the Pharisees were open to God's

activity, they would know that God is active right
among them in Jesus' teaching and deeds, deeds like
that of the cleansing of the lepers (17:11–19).

17:22–25 Harassed as they are, Christians long for
the vindication which the glorious coming of Jesus,
the Son of Man, will effect. Some of their number raise
their anxiety level by proclaiming that the Son of Man
has already come (17:23). Christians are not to go
scurrying hither and yon after them like stock inves-
tors who change all their plans at the slightest whisper
of a "tip." They should not make the same mistake as
the Pharisees and try to capture the inside track on
God's timetable for the end (see 17:20–21). The Son
of Man will come unexpectedly—like lightning. One
facet, though, of the coming of the Son of Man is not
unexpected: His community will share his fate of suffering and rejection (17:25).

17:26–30 Comparisons shed additional light on
Luke's solution to the problem of the coming of the
Son of Man. During the times of Noah and Lot people
were engaged in the everyday human activities of eating, drinking, marrying, and selling. Everything was
fine; why change and repent? Noah and Lot read the
situation quite differently. They were prepared for the
unexpected judgment. Christians, take note.

17:31–37 Just because two people live together or
work side by side is no guarantee that both are prepared for the sudden coming of the Son of Man
(17:34–35). The best preparation for Jesus' coming
is to lose one's life for the sake of others. In that, is
life (17:33). Jesus brushes aside the disciples' snoopy
question about the where of his coming with a prov-

erb: Judgment will be as inevitable as the gathering of vultures around a corpse (17:37).

18:1–8 The refrain of "justice" unifies this passage (18:3, 5, 7, 8). Luke uses the parable of the persistent widow to exhort his church to pray day and night for the Lord's justice. When the Lord delays in coming to do justice to his severely persecuted faithful (18:7), they should not lose heart (18:1). If the self-centered judge granted justice to the helpless widow, how much more will a gracious God grant justice to the beleaguered believers of the Son of Man!

Luke's solution to the when of Jesus' coming avoids the deep end of trying to read God's mind and stresses what the Christian must do to be prepared. As the Christians of Luke's community wait for the coming of Jesus, they must not chase after rumors that he has already come and change their plans of steadfast adherence to him. Nor should they be lulled into thinking that the assured rhythms of everyday life render the need for repentance obsolete. While yearning and praying to be liberated from persecution by Jesus' coming, they must continue to give of themselves, for that is the only sure way they have of preserving their lives.

STUDY QUESTION: Would Luke's solution to the when of Jesus' coming be enthusiastically welcomed by those who see every earthquake, terrorist's bomb, and civil war as a sure sign of the end?

Luke 18:9–14
GOD LOVES SINNERS

9 He spoke the following parable to some people who prided themselves on being virtuous and de-
10 spised everyone else, ·"Two men went up to the Temple to pray, one a Pharisee, the other a tax
11 collector. ·The Pharisee stood there and said this prayer to himself, 'I thank you, God, that I am not grasping, unjust, adulterous like the rest of mankind, and particularly that I am not like this
12 tax collector here. ·I fast twice a week; I pay
13 tithes on all I get.' ·The tax collector stood some distance away, not daring even to raise his eyes to heaven; but he beat his breast and said, 'God,
14 be merciful to me, a sinner.' ·This man, I tell you, went home again at rights with God; the other did not. For everyone who exalts himself will be hum-bled, but the man who humbles himself will be exalted."

✠

The tax collector is the key figure in this popular parable. He was a shady character, despised as a trai-tor by the Jews, and tainted by the filthy lucre he amassed from his bag of customhouse dirty tricks. He was easily classified with the "grasping, unjust, and adulterous" (18:11). To use a popular image, he was decked out in a black hat. The Pharisee wears the white chapeau of super-virtue.

The parable teaches that God loves those in black hats. He accepts the villain and rejects the saint. If you yelled, "Wait a minute!" to this interpretation, then you have felt some of the shock this parable touched off in Jesus' contemporaries. The virtue-laden Pharisee, hero of the people, is rejected. Through Jesus' ministry God gives a warm embrace to the breast-beating tax collector, the people's prize tar-and-feather candidate.

Luke provides an updated version of this powerful parable by adding verse 9 as its introduction: "He spoke the following parable to some people who prided themselves on being virtuous and despised everyone else." The targets of his updating are those paragons of virtue in his community who think they have a corner on sanctity (see chapter 15). Virtue, no matter how dearly bought by self-sacrifice and pain, does not grant the Christian the title of "I saved myself" nor does it elevate him to the rank of despiser of the mini-virtuous.

STUDY QUESTION: Many Christians take stock of their standing before God by tallying their religious observances and devotions. Does this parable issue an order to desist from such a practice?

Luke 18:15-30
AND NOW A FEW WORDS ON "THE GOOD LIFE"

¹⁵ People even brought little children to him, for him to touch them; but when the disciples saw ¹⁶ this they turned them away. ·But Jesus called the children to him and said, "Let the little children come to me, and do not stop them; for it is to such ¹⁷ as these that the kingdom of God belongs. ·I tell you solemnly, anyone who does not welcome the kingdom of God like a little child will never enter it."

¹⁸ A member of one of the leading families put this question to him, "Good Master, what have I ¹⁹ to do to inherit eternal life?" ·Jesus said to him, "Why do you call me good? No one is good but ²⁰ God alone. ·You know the commandments: You must not commit adultery; You must not kill; You must not steal; You must not bring false witness; ²¹ Honor your father and mother." ·He replied, "I have kept all these from my earliest days till ²² now." ·And when Jesus heard this he said, "There is still one thing you lack. Sell all that you own and distribute the money to the poor, and you will have treasure in heaven; then come, follow me." ²³ But when he heard this he was filled with sadness, for he was very rich.

²⁴ Jesus looked at him and said, "How hard it is for those who have riches to make their way into ²⁵ the kingdom of God! ·Yes, it is easier for a camel to pass through the eye of a needle than for a rich ²⁶ man to enter the kingdom of God." ·"In that case," said the listeners, "who can be saved?" ²⁷ "Things that are impossible for men," he replied, "are possible for God."

28 Then Peter said, "What about us? We left all
29 we had to follow you." ·He said to them, "I tell
you solemnly, there is no one who has left house,
wife, brothers, parents or children for the sake of
30 the kingdom of God ·who will not be given repayment many times over in this present time and, in
the world to come, eternal life."

✠

Jesus warmly welcomes the little children. He does
not set them forth as examples of virtue, for they are
not mature enough in life's battles to have won medals
of virtue. They are compelling examples of the dependence and trust in God required of disciples and
stand in sharp contrast to the Pharisee who trusted
exaltedly in himself (18:9–14). This teaching about
dependence and trust in God also anticipates Jesus'
sayings about possessions in verses 18–30.

Luke 18:18–23 is a recognition story: Through
dialogue or an event a person recognizes something
about himself that he did not know before. For example, a person may boast that he does not use foul
language. While being victimized by rush-hour traffic
on an expressway, he recognizes himself as the winner
of the swear award of the week. The rich aristocrat
prides himself on his virtue: I have kept all these commandments from childhood till now. When Jesus asks
him to sell all and become his disciple, he recognizes
something about himself that he had not known previously—he is attached to his possessions. He cannot
say "Yes" to Jesus. Luke's advice to the well-to-do in
his community is challenging: Give yourselves this
same recognition test; do your possessions stand in the
way of your adherence to Jesus?

As the very rich aristocrat stands by, Luke uses

Jesus' sayings to handle further facets of the problem of riches (18:24–27). Riches are a grave hindrance to salvation and are not a sign of God's blessings. God's grace is absolutely necessary for possessors to outdo the feat of a camel passing through the eye of a needle.

After the largely negative admonitions of verses 18–23 and 24–27, Luke now gives positive advice to the well-heeled within his community (18:28–30). These possessors should follow the example of Peter and the apostles, who left what they had to follow Jesus (18:28; the "all" in the translation overinterprets the original Greek). Their example is further clarified in Acts 4:32, 34–35, which describes the ideal early Christian community: "The whole group of believers was united, heart and soul; no one claimed for his own use *anything that he had.* . . . None of their members was ever in want, as all those who owned land or houses would sell them, and bring the money from them, to present it to the apostles; it was then distributed to any members who might be in need." The rich should ensure that no one in the Christian community is in need.

Luke's message, then, to the possessors is basically twofold: detachment from possessions; charity toward those in need.

STUDY QUESTION: Darling children and rich folk. How do we prevent our children, who grow up in a consumerism-crazed society, from becoming addicted to "the good life" and blinded to the needy?

Luke 18:31–43
PERSISTENT DISCIPLESHIP

31 Then taking the Twelve aside he said to them, "Now we are going up to Jerusalem, and everything that is written by the prophets about the 32 Son of Man is to come true. ·For he will be handed over to the pagans and will be mocked, maltreated 33 and spat on, ·and when they have scourged him they will put him to death; and on the third day he 34 will rise again." ·But they could make nothing of this; what he said was quite obscure to them, they had no idea what it meant.

35 Now as he drew near to Jericho there was a blind man sitting at the side of the road begging. 36 When he heard the crowd going past he asked 37 what it was all about, ·and they told him that Jesus 38 the Nazarene was passing by. ·So he called out, 39 "Jesus, Son of David, have pity on me." ·The people in front scolded him and told him to keep quiet, but he shouted all the louder, "Son of 40 David, have pity on me." ·Jesus stopped and ordered them to bring the man to him, and when 41 he came up, asked him, ·"What do you want me to do for you?" "Sir," he replied, "let me see 42 again." ·Jesus said to him, "Receive your sight. 43 Your faith has saved you." ·And instantly his sight returned and he followed him praising God, and all the people who saw it gave praise to God for what had happened.

✠

In this section Luke unfurls the final passion prediction of his travel narrative. Jerusalem is not only the goal of pilgrim Jesus; it is also the place where

martyrs are killed. By adding "by the prophets" in
18:31, Luke taps into another rich theme of his:
Jesus' death was forewilled by God (see also 9:22;
22:37; 24:25–27, 32, 44–47; Ac 2:22–26; 3:12–26).

In our commentary on the travel narrative we have
been observing that the miracles Luke preserves there
do not so much underline Jesus' power to heal as serve
as vehicles for his teaching. The miracle at hand is no
exception. The people inform the blind man that the
commotion is caused by the arrival of Jesus the
Nazarene. The blind man's faith already surfaces in
his confession, "Jesus, Son of David, have pity on me,"
which goes beyond what the crowd had told him about
Jesus. Despite the attempts to silence him, he persists
in his faith. In his mercy Jesus performs an act of the
Messiah, Son of David, and gives him sight (see Is
29:18, Lk 7:22). If the miracle story ended here,
Jesus' power to cure would be at center stage. But for
the first and only time in all his miracle stories Luke
writes that the cured man *follows Jesus*. He is not
following Jesus as a happy puppy would follow someone who gave him a tasty hunk of meat. His following
is the loving response of discipleship.

Luke tells his fellow travelers on Jesus' way that
God has acted for them in Jesus (18:43). Their response to that gracious activity must be persistent,
faithful following of the one who went up to Jerusalem
and his death.

STUDY QUESTION: "Persistent, faithful following of
Jesus" is so frequent a Lukan
theme that it can roll like jargon
from our lips. What ingredients
characterize persistent and faithful
discipleship?

Luke 19:1-10
MERCY FOR THE RICH,
REPENTANT ZACCHAEUS

19 ¹He entered Jericho and was going through
²the town ·when a man whose name was
Zacchaeus made his appearance; he was one of
³the senior tax collectors and a wealthy man. ·He
was anxious to see what kind of man Jesus was,
but he was too short and could not see him for
⁴the crowd; ·so he ran ahead and climbed a syca-
more tree to catch a glimpse of Jesus who was
⁵to pass that way. ·When Jesus reached the spot
he looked up and spoke to him: "Zacchaeus,
come down. Hurry, because I must stay at your
⁶house today." ·And he hurried down and wel-
⁷comed him joyfully. ·They all complained when
they saw what was happening. "He has gone to
⁸stay at a sinner's house," they said. ·But Zacchaeus stood his ground and said to the Lord,
"Look, sir, I am going to give half my property to
the poor, and if I have cheated anybody I will
⁹pay him back four times the amount." ·And Jesus
said to him, "Today salvation has come to this
house, because this man too is a son of Abraham;
¹⁰for the Son of Man has come to seek out and save
what was lost."

✠

In this section the master artist Luke gives greater
detail and depth to his dual portraits of Jesus—friend
of outcasts, champion of the poor.

Verses 7 and 8 unlock the interpretation of this
story. Verse 7 reads: "He has gone to stay at a *sinner's
house*." Tax collectors like Zacchaeus were despised

by their fellow Jews because of their dishonesty in collecting duties. Deprived of civic rights, they were considered "sinners."

Verse 8 is Luke's modification of this story, which he inherited from tradition. For in verse 9 Jesus addresses Zacchaeus not in the second person, but in the third person; verse 9 would actually follow more smoothly after verse 7. Further, in verse 8 Jesus is addressed by the postresurrection title of Lord. Finally, verse 8 accords with the favorite Lukan theme of repentance (see 5:32, where Luke has modified a similar story by the insertion of "to repentance"). The traditional story without verse 8, emphasized the unconditional and gratuitous nature of Jesus' offer of mercy. In Jesus' eyes Zacchaeus was not a sinner—a religious and social outcast. By his joyful response to Jesus' invitation to table fellowship, Zacchaeus shows that he is a son of Abraham.

In recognizing that verse 8 contains Luke's theology, the reader is granted a peek into the church life of Luke's time, when Jesus' message of unconditional mercy had entered into dialogue with the ongoing church's experience and life. While Luke's church remains true to Jesus' message of unconditional mercy, it must also be assured of the commitment of rich Christians lest Jesus' call becomes cheap grace and be offered at bargain-basement prices.

Luke also uses verse 8 as a contrast to the story of the rich aristocrat in 18:18–30 and thereby shows that he doesn't have a pat answer to the problems created for his church by the presence of rich Christians. Zacchaeus doesn't give all his possessions to the poor (see 18:22)—just half. He avoids the pitfall of wealth (18:24–27) and shares what he has with those in need (18:28–30).

STUDY QUESTIONS: In the dialogue about God's mercy have Christians espoused Luke's side more often than Jesus'? Do we say, Sure, Jesus' mercy is unconditional, but we must first assure ourselves that you qualify to receive it?

11 While the people were listening to this he went
on to tell a parable, because he was near Jerusalem and they imagined that the kingdom of God
12 was going to show itself then and there. ·Accord-
ingly he said, "A man of noble birth went to a
distant country to be appointed king and after-
13 ward return. ·He summoned ten of his servants
and gave them ten pounds. 'Do business with
14 these,' he told them, 'until I get back.' ·But his
compatriots detested him and sent a delegation
to follow him with this message, 'We do not want
this man to be our king.'

15 "Now on his return, having received his ap-
pointment as king, he sent for those servants to
whom he had given the money, to find out what
16 profit each had made. ·The first came in and said,
17 'Sir, your one pound has brought in ten.' ·'Well
done, my good servant!' he replied. 'Since you
have proved yourself faithful in a very small thing,
18 you shall have the government of ten cities.' ·Then
came the second and said, 'Sir, your one pound
19 has made five.' ·To this one also he said, 'And you
20 shall be in charge of five cities.' ·Next came the
other and said, 'Sir, here is your pound. I put it
21 away safely in a piece of linen ·because I was
afraid of you; for you are an exacting man: you
pick up what you have not put down and reap
22 what you have not sown.' ·'You wicked servant!'
he said. 'Out of your own mouth I condemn you.
So you knew I was an exacting man, picking up
what I have not put down and reaping what I have
23 not sown? ·Then why did you not put my money
in the bank? On my return I could have drawn it

24 out with interest.' ·And he said to those standing
by, 'Take the pound from him and give it to the
25 man who has ten pounds.' ·And they said to him,
26 'But, sir, he has ten pounds . . .' ·'I tell you, to
everyone who has will be given more; but from
the man who has not, even what he has will be
taken away.

27   " 'But as for my enemies who did not want me
for their king, bring them here and execute them
in my presence.' "

✠

Jesus' parable of the pounds was not only remembered by the early Christian community, but also re-
interpreted for new generations. This reverent reinterpretation has caused bumps in the smooth road of the
parable. One of the biggest bumps is the interweaving
of the parable of the rejected king with that of the
pounds (see 19:12, 14, 15a, 27).

Luke further reinterprets the parable he inherited
from tradition by decking it out with an introduction
(19:11) and by the words "do business with these"
(19:13) and "to find out what profit each had made"
(19:15). Luke insists that Jesus' role was not to establish an earthly kingdom in Jerusalem (19:11).
While Jesus is absent from the community, it is paramount that his disciples parlay what he has entrusted
to them (19:13, 15); for when he returns, he will not
honor the excuse of the disobedient and unproductive
servant (19:22). Learn from those who rejected King
Jesus and were judged in the destruction of Jerusalem
(19:27).

Underneath the various layers of reinterpretation,
the constant focal point of the parable of the pounds
is the third servant. He is a tragic figure, who is fully
cognizant that the money he has belongs to someone

else who expects a return on his capital and yet is im-
mobilized at the mere hint of taking a risk, and tucks
the money away for safekeeping in a piece of linen.
Such a servant is stripped of his trust.

This tragic figure is not so much an individual as it is
Israel or the church. It is not enough for Israel or the
church to strive to preserve what they have received
from God. They must show a profit on the capital entrusted to them. Concretely, this means that neither
Israel nor the Christian community can erect a huge,
protective fence around God's revelation. They must
welcome new words from God's prophets and messengers; they must bring God's message to different peoples and climes. All told, the parable does not simply
exhort Christians to use their personal talents profitably; hundreds of other teachers have said as much.
The message is religious: Those entrusted with God's
revelation cannot guard it in a museum or make it
windproof to the breath of God's Spirit. They must
make that revelation yield dividends by venturing forth
with it into changed times and foreign cultures.

STUDY QUESTION: God's revelation cannot be handed
                  on in some antiseptic, ecclesiastical
                  pouch. How can Christians get
                  more deeply involved in the high-
                  risk task of setting forth the mean-
                  ing of God's revelation for a new
                  generation?

JESUS IS FOR PEACE

28 When he had said this he went on ahead, going
29 up to Jerusalem. ·Now when he was near Beth-
phage and Bethany, close by the Mount of Olives
as it is called, he sent two of the disciples, telling
30 them, ·"Go off to the village opposite, and as you
enter it you will find a tethered colt that no one
31 has yet ridden. Untie it and bring it here. ·If anyone asks you, 'Why are you untying it?' you are
32 to say this, 'The Master needs it.'" ·The messengers went off and found everything just as he had
33 told them. ·As they were untying the colt, its
owner said, "Why are you untying that colt?"
34 and they answered, "The Master needs it."
35 So they took the colt to Jesus, and throwing
their garments over its back they helped Jesus
36 onto it. ·As he moved off, people spread their
37 cloaks in the road, ·and now, as he was approach-
ing the downward slope of the Mount of Olives,
the whole group of disciples joyfully began to
praise God at the top of their voices for all the
38 miracles they had seen. ·They cried out:

> "Blessings on the King who comes,
> in the name of the Lord!
> Peace in heaven
> and glory in the highest heavens!"

39 Some Pharisees in the crowd said to him, "Mas-
40 ter, check your disciples," ·but he answered, "I
tell you, if these keep silence the stones will cry
out."
41 As he drew near and came in sight of the city
42 he shed tears over it ·and said, "If you in your
turn had only understood on this day the message

of peace! But, alas, it is hidden from your eyes!
⁴³ Yes, a time is coming when your enemies will
raise fortifications all around you, when they will
⁴⁴ encircle you and hem you in on every side; ·they
will dash you and the children inside your walls to
the ground; they will leave not one stone standing
on another within you—and all because you did
not recognize your opportunity when God offered
it!"

☩

With this Palm Sunday Gospel Luke concludes his
travel narrative and builds upon the rejected-king
theme of the preceding section (19:12, 14, 15a, 27).
The whole group of disciples hails Jesus as king
(19:38), for they acknowledge his miracles as signs
of his kingly rule over those enemies of peace—sickness, demons, and death (19:37; see 4:18, 7:21–22).
All Jewish hopes to the contrary notwithstanding,
Jesus' kingly rule is for peace—peace in the compre-
hensive sense of physical and spiritual wholeness and
well-being (19:38, 42)—not for war. As a sign of his
peaceful rule, Jesus the King eschews a warhorse and
rides on the colt of a lowly donkey. By doing so, he
fulfills the prophet Zechariah's prediction of the
messianic king: "Rejoice heart and soul, daughter of
Zion! Shout with gladness, daughter of Jerusalem! See
now, your king comes to you; he is victorious, he is
triumphant, humble and riding on a donkey, on a colt,
the foal of a donkey" (Zc 9:9).

Yet Jesus, the peace-bringing king, is rejected. The
opposition Jesus encountered during his Galilean
ministry and journey to Jerusalem reaches its climax
here in Jerusalem (19:39, 41–44). In Jerusalem Jesus
will continue to prophesy and teach against the reli-

gious powers-that-be (19:45 to 21:38). Although God was present in the peace-effecting teaching and deeds of Jesus the King, such a king did not fit into Jerusalem's plans (19:44).

Besides giving a capsule message on the kingly rule of Messiah-Jesus, Luke has another intention in this section: to contrast the persistent faith of the blind man who follows Jesus (18:35–43) with the blindness of the Jerusalem authorities (19:42). Luke asks his fellow Christians whether they will close their eyes to the many manifestations of God's peace they have experienced. The Jewish religious leaders show that such blindness is no respecter of persons.

STUDY QUESTION: This section presents a classic case of the reality of fulfillment conflicting with people's expectations of it. How do we cope when God's action or nonaction fails to accord with our hopes and desires?

Jesus in Jerusalem:
Final Teaching and Rejection
Luke 19:45 to 23:56

Introduction to Luke 19:45 to 23:56
JESUS IN JERUSALEM:
FINAL TEACHING AND REJECTION

In these chapters Luke's goal is not to provide an exact description of Jesus' last words and days. His interest lies elsewhere; he uses the traditions he has inherited to buoy up his church's faith. He accomplishes this by bringing to well-rounded conclusions themes he has developed in the course of his Gospel. A preview of these themes will help us spot them when they occur.

The theme of Jesus, the peaceful *king,* culminates in the startling picture of Jesus, the crucified king. "The soldiers mocked him too, and when they approached to offer him vinegar they said, 'If you are the king of the Jews, save yourself.' Above him there was an inscription: 'This is the King of the Jews'" (23:36–38). To his last breath Jesus continues his *kingly ministry to the sinner* and saves the "good thief" (23:40–43).

Jesus, who taught God's will in Galilee and on his journey to Jerusalem, exercises his kingly rule by *teaching daily in the Temple.* "He taught in the Temple every day. The chief priests tried to do away with him, but they did not see how they could carry this out because the people as a whole hung on his words" (19:47–48). The people flock to hear him while *the religious leaders reject him.*

Even though Jesus is persecuted and rejected by the religious authorities, he is *innocent.* Herod and Pilate declare him innocent (23:14–15), and the Roman centurion at the cross exclaims that Jesus was certainly innocent (23:47).

These chapters are specially important for Luke's innocent church as it carries out its commission of teaching in the throes of persecution.

JESUS, GOD'S PRESENCE
AMONG HIS PEOPLE

45 Then he went into the Temple and began
46 driving out those who were selling. ·"According
to scripture," he said, "my house will be a house
of prayer. But you have turned it into a robbers'
den."

47 He taught in the Temple every day. The chief
priests and the scribes, with the support of the
48 leading citizens, tried to do away with him, ·but
they did not see how they could carry this out
because the people as a whole hung on his words.

1   20 Now one day while he was teaching the
people in the Temple and proclaiming the
Good News, the chief priests and the scribes
2 came up, together with the elders, ·and spoke to
him. "Tell us," they said, "what authority have
you for acting like this? Or who is it that gave you
3 this authority?" ·"And I," replied Jesus, "will ask
4 you a question. Tell me: ·John's baptism: did it
5 come from heaven, or from man?" ·And they
argued it out this way among themselves, "If we
say from heaven, he will say, 'Why did you refuse
6 to believe him?'; ·and if we say from man, the
people will all stone us, for they are convinced
7 that John was a prophet." ·So their reply was
8 that they did not know where it came from. ·And
Jesus said to them, "Nor will I tell you my authority for acting like this."

9 And he went on to tell the people this parable:
"A man planted a vineyard and leased it to ten-
10 ants, and went abroad for a long while. ·When the
time came, he sent a servant to the tenants to get

his share of the produce of the vineyard from
them. But the tenants thrashed him, and sent him
11 away empty-handed. ·But he persevered and sent
a second servant; they thrashed him too and
treated him shamefully and sent him away empty-
12 handed. ·He still persevered and sent a third; they
13 wounded this one also, and threw him out. ·Then
the owner of the vineyard said, 'What am I to
do? I will send them my dear son. Perhaps they
14 will respect him.' ·But when the tenants saw him
they put their heads together. 'This is the heir,'
they said, 'let us kill him so that the inheritance
15 will be ours.' ·So they threw him out of the vineyard and killed him.

"Now what will the owner of the vineyard do
16 to them? ·He will come and make an end of these
tenants and give the vineyard to others." Hearing
17 this they said, "God forbid!" ·But he looked hard
at them and said, "Then what does this text in the
scriptures mean:

It was the stone rejected by the builders
that became the keystone?

18 Anyone who falls on that stone will be dashed to
pieces; anyone it falls on will be crushed."
19   But for their fear of the people, the scribes and
the chief priests would have liked to lay hands on
him that very moment, because they realized that
this parable was aimed at them.

✠

Writing after the faith-rattling destruction of God's
Temple in A.D. 70, Luke faces the problem of the
significance of that event. In this section he deals with
that problem by illuminating Jesus' relationship to the
Temple and to its demise.

We can get a good clue to what Luke is after if we
think ourselves back into the first century A.D. and recall that the Temple is not some tourist attraction

which lures tens of thousands of gaping camera-toters each year. This magnificent edifice is the place and symbol of God's presence among his people. It is more. It is the center of the Jewish cult and the goal of the annual religious pilgrimages. In the Temple, God's will, revealed in the Law, is preserved and taught.

The Temple was all this, but a glance through the prophetic books of the Old Testament shows that it was constantly in need of reform. For example, the prophet Jeremiah upbraids the worshipers of his time: "Listen to the word of Yahweh, all of you men of Judah who come in by these gates to worship Yahweh. Yahweh Sabaoth, the God of Israel, says this: Amend your behavior and your actions and I will stay with you here in this place. . . . Steal, would you, murder, commit adultery, perjure yourselves, burn incense to Baal, follow alien gods that you do not know?—and then come presenting yourselves in this Temple that bears my name, saying: Now we are safe—safe to go on committing all these abominations! Do you take this Temple that bears my name for a *robbers' den?*" (7:2–3, 9–11; see Lk 19:46). Prophets who taught after Jeremiah's death announced that the longed-for permanent reform of the Temple would occur in the days of the Messiah.

With the above background in mind we can appreciate the fact that nowhere in 19:28–48 does Luke say that Jesus entered Jerusalem. In 19:45 he notes very explicitly that Jesus entered the Temple—but does not mention Jerusalem. By means of this subtle change of his source, Mark 11:15, Luke gives prime-time billing to Jesus' actions in the Temple. When he casts out the sellers, Jesus performs a messianic act of Temple renewal. Further light is shed on this dramatic action from the description of Temple renewal found in one of the later prophets, Zechariah: "There will be no more traders in the Temple of Yahweh Sabaoth, when that day comes" (Zc 14:21). Luke builds upon the Old Testament teaching about God's Temple and teaches that Jesus is God's renewing presence within the Temple.

Jesus' reform of the Temple is not restricted to expelling the money-makers; he also reforms it by performing a function which had been neglected—he teaches God's will in the Temple (19:47 to 20:1). The implications of these dual acts of reform are not lost on the religious leaders, who question him: "What authority have you for acting like this? Or who is it that gave you this authority?" (20:2). Jesus will not be duped by their intrigue and counters with a question of his own. The Jerusalem religious authorities, the Sanhedrin, reveal the same blindness to God's will as the Galilean Pharisees and lawyers. And the people—God's people—are open to Jesus and hang on his every word (20:6).

Luke utilizes a parable, drawn from the real life Palestinian situation of absentee landowners and rascally defaulting tenants, to further illumine Jesus' relationship to the Temple and to its destruction. Time after time the religious leaders have failed to recognize God's authority in his servants the prophets and have not given fruit to their rightful owner. They even reject the authority of God's final messenger, his dear beloved Son, by throwing him outside the walls of the vineyard and killing him (recall that Jesus is crucified outside the walls of Jerusalem). For rejecting the beloved Son, the tenants will be severely punished, and the vineyard will be given over to others. The people of God, the primary audience of the parable (20:9), do not want this to happen and cry out "God forbid!"

(20:16). They are not responsible for Jesus' rejection. It is the fault of their religious leaders that the city of Jerusalem and its Temple are destroyed. Although the beloved Son is rejected, he will be vindicated by God and become the keystone in God's new building. And as 20:18 states so graphically, Jesus destroys those who reject him.

Luke employs the events of Jesus' life to comment on the significance of the destruction of God's Temple in A.D. 70. Jesus' messianic claims to be God's renewing presence among his people meet with concerted opposition and ultimate rejection from the religious authorities. Because of their continued blindness to God's messengers, these leaders and their Temple are rejected. The destruction of God's Temple, however, does not spell the end of God's presence among his people. The people of God, who reform their lives and believe in Jesus, are a spiritual temple built upon the keystone of the risen Jesus.

STUDY QUESTION: How can contemporary Christians escape from the temptations of assuming that God's presence among them is a matter of stones and mortar and that they are owners, rather than tenants, of God's gifts to them?

Luke 20:20–44
THE NATURE OF THE
MESSIAH-KING, JESUS

²⁰ So they waited their opportunity and sent agents to pose as men devoted to the Law, and to fasten on something he might say and so enable them to hand him over to the jurisdiction and ²¹ authority of the governor. ·They put to him this question, "Master, we know that you say and teach what is right; you favor no one, but teach ²² the way of God in all honesty. ·Is it permissible ²³ for us to pay taxes to Caesar or not?" ·But he was ²⁴ aware of their cunning and said, ·"Show me a denarius. Whose head and name are on it?" ²⁵ "Caesar's," they said. ·"Well then," he said to them, "give back to Caesar what belongs to Caesar—and to God what belongs to God."

²⁶ As a result, they were unable to find fault with anything he had to say in public; his answer took them by surprise and they were silenced.

²⁷ Some Sadducees—those who say that there is no resurrection—approached him and they put this ²⁸ question to him, ·"Master, we have it from Moses in writing, that if a man's married brother dies childless, the man must marry the widow to raise ²⁹ up children for his brother. ·Well then, there were seven brothers. The first, having married a wife, ³⁰₃₁ died childless. ·The second ·and then the third married the widow. And the same with all seven, ³² they died leaving no children. ·Finally the woman ³³ herself died. ·Now, at the resurrection, to which of them will she be wife since she had been married to all seven?"

³⁴ Jesus replied, "The children of this world take ³⁵ wives and husbands, ·but those who are judged

36 worthy of a place in the other world and in the
resurrection from the dead do not marry ·because
they can no longer die, for they are the same as
the angels, and being children of the resurrection
37 they are sons of God. ·And Moses himself implies
that the dead rise again, in the passage about the
bush where he calls the Lord the God of Abraham, the God of Isaac and the God of Jacob.
38 Now he is God, not of the dead, but of the living;
for to him all men are in fact alive."

39   Some scribes then spoke up. "Well put, Mas-
40 ter," they said ·—because they would not dare to
ask him any more questions.

41   He then said to them, "How can people main-
42 tain that the Christ is son of David? ·Why, David
himself says in the Book of Psalms:

> The Lord said to my Lord:
> Sit at my right hand
43 > and I will make your enemies
> a footstool for you.

44 David here calls him Lord; how then can he be his
son?"

✠

In this section Jesus' opponents turn his public
teaching in the Temple into a press conference and
pommel him with loaded questions.

Jesus brilliantly parries the question of those who
want to paint him into the corner of opposing the
Roman occupational forces (20:20–26). The very
fact that his questioners have a Roman denarius on
their persons indicates that they acknowledge the
ruler of those who issue such coins. Jesus tells them
to give those rulers what they require, but don't forget
to give God his due. Although this passage very clearly
shows that Jesus is no revolutionary freedom-fighter,
his opponents later use this controversy in their accusa-

tion of Jesus before Pilate: "We found this man inciting our people to revolt, opposing payment of the
tribute to Caesar, and claiming to be Christ, a king"
(23:2).

The Sadducees follow up with their own ear-
catching question (20:27–39). Their attempt to re-
duce Jesus' teaching to ridicule backfires, for Jesus ex-
plains that "the other world" (20:35) isn't concerned
about propagating the human race as this world is, for
people do not die there. Jesus' God is a God of the
living, not of the dead. Through this passage we
glimpse Jesus' trust in the God who will raise him
from the dead. By adding 20:38b, "for to him all men
are in fact alive," to his source, Mark 12:27; Luke
teaches that Christians have this same hope of resurrection because they already now share in the resurrection life.

Jesus' answers leave his opponents scurrying for the
exits (20:40). It remains for Jesus to clarify the
Davidic nature of the Messiah (20:41–44). The
Messiah—Jesus—is more exalted than King David because he is David's Lord and Master.

In this section Luke underscores some very important aspects of Jesus' role as Messiah: He is no political revolutionary; he will not remain in death's grasp,
for the God of the living will raise him up; he is not
only David's son but also his Lord.

STUDY QUESTION: Does the fact that Jesus was not a
political revolutionary mean that
his followers must be pacifists or
remain passive in the face of governmental oppression and injustice?

Luke 20:45 to 21:4
SERVICE IS THE CLERGY'S
MOST IMPORTANT PRODUCT

45 While all the people were listening he said to the
46 disciples, ·"Beware of the scribes who like to walk
about in long robes and love to be greeted obsequiously in the market squares, to take the front
seats in the synagogues and the places of honor
47 at banquets, ·who swallow the property of widows,
while making a show of lengthy prayers. The more
severe will be the sentence they receive."

1 **21** As he looked up he saw rich people putting
2 their offerings into the treasury; ·then he
happened to notice a poverty-stricken widow
3 putting in two small coins, ·and he said, "I tell
you truly, this poor widow has put in more than
4 any of them; ·for these have all contributed money
they had over, but she from the little she had has
put in all she had to live on."

✠

In this section Luke follows his source, Mark
12:38–44, very closely. He does, however, make one
significant modification in his introduction. Mark
writes: "In his teaching he said, 'Beware of the
scribes'" (Mk 12:38). Luke has: "While all the people were listening he said *to the disciples,* 'Beware of
the scribes'" (20:45).

Luke directs these instructions to the disciples, the
church leaders of his own day. They should not model
their leadership on that of the scribes, whose main con-

cern was advertising their importance. As Luke has insisted (12:41–48) and will insist later on in his Gospel (22:24–27), Christian leadership is for service to others, not for self-aggrandizement. The puzzling "who swallow the property of widows" refers to the scribes' habit of sponging off the hospitality of widows and literally eating them out of house and home.

The extraordinarily generous widow gives everything she has to further the worship of God. Her two small coins are the least in value and perhaps equal two cents. Luke confronts the church leaders of his day with her example. They must be willing to make as many sacrifices as she did to serve God.

STUDY QUESTION: Clergy are often put on pedestals by lay people. Are church leaders to blame when such deference causes the disease of ego inflation and creates expectations for red-carpet treatment?

Luke 21:5–38
THE DESTRUCTION OF JERUSALEM IS NOT THE END OF THE WORLD

5 When some were talking about the Temple, remarking how it was adorned with fine stonework
6 and votive offerings, he said, ·"All these things you are staring at now—the time will come when not a single stone will be left on another: every-
7 thing will be destroyed." ·And they put to him this question: "Master," they said, "when will this happen, then, and what sign will there be that this is about to take place?"
8 "Take care not to be deceived," he said, "because many will come using my name and saying, 'I am he,' and, 'The time is near at hand.' Refuse
9 to join them. ·And when you hear of wars and revolutions, do not be frightened, for this is something that must happen but the end is not so
10 soon." ·Then he said to them, "Nation will fight against nation, and kingdom against kingdom.
11 There will be great earthquakes and plagues and famines here and there; there will be fearful sights and great signs from heaven.
12 "But before all this happens, men will seize you and persecute you; they will hand you over to the synagogues and to imprisonment, and bring you before kings and governors because of my name
13 —and that will be your opportunity to bear wit-
14 ness. ·Keep this carefully in mind: you are not to
15 prepare your defense, ·because I myself shall give you an eloquence and a wisdom that none of your opponents will be able to resist or contradict.
16 You will be betrayed even by parents and brothers, relations and friends; and some of you will be
17 put to death. ·You will be hated by all men on ac-

¹⁸ count of my name, ·but not a hair of your head
¹⁹ will be lost. ·Your endurance will win you your
lives.

²⁰   "When you see Jerusalem surrounded by
armies, you must realize that she will soon be laid
²¹ desolate. ·Then those in Judaea must escape to the
mountains, those inside the city must leave it, and
those in country districts must not take refuge in
²² it. ·For this is the time of vengeance when all that
²³ scripture says must be fulfilled. ·Alas for those
with child, or with babies at the breast, when
those days come!

"For great misery will descend on the land and
²⁴ wrath on this people. ·They will fall by the edge
of the sword and be led captive to every pagan
country; and Jerusalem will be trampled down
by the pagans until the age of the pagans is completely over.

²⁵   "There will be signs in the sun and moon and
stars; on earth nations in agony, bewildered by the
²⁶ clamor of the ocean and its waves; ·men dying of
fear as they await what menaces the world, for
²⁷ the powers of heaven will be shaken. ·And then
they will see the Son of Man coming in a cloud
²⁸ with power and great glory. ·When these things
begin to take place, stand erect, hold your heads
high, because your liberation is near at hand."

²⁹   And he told them a parable, "Think of the fig
³⁰ tree and indeed every tree. ·As soon as you see
them bud, you know that summer is now near.
³¹ So with you when you see these things happening:
³² know that the kingdom of God is near. ·I tell you
solemnly, before this generation has passed away
³³ all will have taken place. ·Heaven and earth will
pass away, but my words will never pass away.

³⁴   "Watch yourselves, or your hearts will be
coarsened with debauchery and drunkenness and
the cares of life, and that day will be sprung on
³⁵ you suddenly, ·like a trap. For it will come down
³⁶ on every living man on the face of the earth. ·Stay
awake, praying at all times for the strength to sur-

vive all that is going to happen, and to stand with
confidence before the Son of Man."

37 In the daytime he would be in the Temple
teaching, but would spend the night on the hill
38 called the Mount of Olives. ·And from early
morning the people would gather around him in
the Temple to listen to him.

✠

Longtime residents of a city can become so attached
to their city that it becomes the hub of their universe.
Destroy that city or move them away, and they become
painfully unhappy and disorientated. In this section
Luke addresses himself to a situation where members
of his community were so attached to the city Jerusalem that it was the center of their universe. When that
city and its Temple were destroyed in A.D. 70, they
were distraught and confused and began to think that
the end of the world had dawned.

An outline of this discourse will help us home in on
Luke's message:

Introduction (21:5–7)
Initial exhortation (21:8–9)
Cosmic disasters (21:10–11)
Things which occur before the end of the
world:
    Christians are persecuted (21:12–19)
    Destruction of Jerusalem (21:20–24)
Cosmic disasters (21:25–33)
Final exhortation (21:34–36)
Conclusion (21:37–38)

The "exhortations" and "cosmic disasters" are
parallel and frame the heart of this discourse: events

which will occur before the end of the world, but which are not themselves signs of the end (21:12–24).

Christians are exhorted not to be stampeded by those who declare that the annihilation of Jerusalem is a sure sign that the coming of the Son of Man is imminent (21:8; see the commentary on 17:22–25 for greater detail).

Luke begins the description of the cosmic disasters in verses 10–11 and interrupts it in verses 12–24, only to resume it in verses 25–33. Why the interruption? The words "but before all this happens" (21:12) are the key to an answer. Before the cosmic disasters—the signs of the end—occur, the events detailed in the interruption will happen.

Persecution is not a sign of the end of the world (21:12–19). As a matter of fact, persecution will be the church's bedfellow for as long as it perdures. Yet such persecution should not cause Christians to lose hope as if they were fighting alone, for Jesus himself will give them an eloquence and a wisdom that none of their opponents will be able to resist or contradict. The destruction of Jerusalem is not a sign of the end of the world (21:20–24). It occurs before the end, whose real signs are listed in verses 25–28.

Luke uses the parable of the fig tree to assure his readers that the end of the world will surely come (21:29–33). "This generation" is that generation of humankind which is alive when the bell tolls for the end of the world.

Exhortations which pick up familiar Lukan themes conclude the discourse (21:34–36). "Debauchery and drunkenness" are the imprint of those servants who lived it up in the absence of their master (12:45). "The cares of life" recall those folk in the days of Noah and Lot who were totally absorbed in the daily concerns of life (17:26–30). "Praying at all times" echoes the parable "about the need to pray continually and never lose heart" (18:1–8).

In summary, Luke insists that the destruction of Jerusalem, while traumatic, is not a sign that the end of the world is around the corner. During the dog days of persecution Christians should be confident that a loving God will not allow a hair of their heads to be lost, for he will preserve their life for eternity. Entanglement in the cares of life will weaken their commitment to the Son of Man, who is going to come at a time determined by God and not by such events as the destruction of Jerusalem.

STUDY QUESTION: Does this section provide contemporary Christians with any program on how to live during the long haul of waiting for the coming of the Son of Man?

Luke 22:1-13
THE DEEPER MEANING OF
JESUS' PASSION

¹ ² **22** The feast of Unleavened Bread, called the Passover, was now drawing near, ·and the chief priests and the scribes were looking for some way of doing away with him, because they mistrusted the people.

³ Then Satan entered into Judas, surnamed Iscariot, who was numbered among the Twelve.
⁴ He went to the chief priests and the officers of the guard to discuss a scheme for handing Jesus over
⁵ to them. ·They were delighted and agreed to give
⁶ him money. ·He accepted, and looked for an opportunity to betray him to them without the people knowing.

⁷ The day of Unleavened Bread came around, the day on which the passover had to be sacrificed,
⁸ and he sent Peter and John, saying, "Go and make the preparations for us to eat the passover."
⁹ "Where do you want us to prepare it?" they asked.
¹⁰ "Listen," he said, "as you go into the city you will meet a man carrying a pitcher of water. Follow
¹¹ him into the house he enters ·and tell the owner of the house, 'The Master has this to say to you: Where is the dining room in which I can eat the
¹² passover with my disciples?' ·The man will show you a large upper room furnished with couches.
¹³ Make the preparations there." ·They set off and found everything as he had told them, and prepared the passover.

✠

In the two scenes of this section we will explore the significance of Luke's modifications of his source, Mark.

Luke's addition of verse 3, "Then Satan entered into Judas," sounds the overture to his entire passion account. Satan, whom Jesus had subdued in his temptations in the desert (4:1–13), resumes his offensive against Jesus. Luke also directs his readers' attention beyond a superficial reading of Jesus' passion and crucifixion as the mere work of hostile religious leaders. Luke 22:53 is highly illuminating in this context: Jesus said, "When I was among you in the Temple day after day you never moved to lay hands on me. But this is your hour; *this is the reign of darkness.*"

The second scene (22:7–13) previews the paramount importance of Jesus' farewell meal with his apostles. Three points stand out in Luke's adaptation of Mark. A comparison will uncover Luke's first two points, which are highlighted by italics:

> His disciples said to him, "Where do you want us to go and make the preparations for you to eat the passover?" (Mk 14:12)

> And *he sent* Peter and John, saying, "Go and make the preparations *for us* to eat the passover" (Lk 22:8)

First, Jesus anticipates his disciples' query and sends two of them; he is in total command of the situation and enters his passion freely and willingly. Second, Jesus' last meal is a meal "for us." Jesus is not a solitary diner; his meal with his apostles has significance for all Christians. Finally, like Mark, Luke depicts Jesus as a powerful prophet. His predictions are fulfilled to

the nth degree (22:13). Such extraordinary power instills confidence in Christians that Jesus' predictions
which dominate 22:14–38, e.g., 22:30, will be fulfilled.

STUDY QUESTION: This section gives Jesus top billing.
                  Who is this Jesus that his last hours
                  command the total attention of
                  Satan?

Luke 22:14–38
JESUS' PRICELESS LEGACY

14 When the hour came he took his place at table,
15 and the apostles with him. ·And he said to them,
"I have longed to eat this passover with you
16 before I suffer; ·because, I tell you, I shall not eat
it again until it is fulfilled in the kingdom of
God."
17 Then, taking a cup, he gave thanks and said,
18 "Take this and share it among you, ·because from
now on, I tell you, I shall not drink wine until the
kingdom of God comes."
19 Then he took some bread and when he had
given thanks, broke it and gave it to them, saying,
"This is my body which will be given for you; do
20 this as a memorial of me." ·He did the same with
the cup after supper, and said, "This cup is the
new covenant in my blood which will be poured
out for you.
21 "And yet, here with me on the table is the hand
22 of the man who betrays me. ·The Son of Man does
indeed go to his fate even as it has been decreed,
but alas for that man by whom he is betrayed!"
23 And they began to ask one another which of them
it could be who was to do this thing.
24 A dispute arose also between them about which
25 should be reckoned the greatest, ·but he said to
them, "Among pagans it is the kings who lord
it over them, and those who have authority over
26 them are given the title Benefactor. ·This must not
happen with you. No; the greatest among you
must behave as if he were the youngest, the
27 leader as if he were the one who serves. ·For who
is the greater: the one at table or the one who

serves? The one at table, surely? Yet here am I
among you as one who serves!

28 "You are the men who have stood by me faith-
29 fully in my trials; ·and now I confer a kingdom on
you, just as my Father conferred one on me:
30 you will eat and drink at my table in my kingdom,
and you will sit on thrones to judge the twelve
tribes of Israel.

31   "Simon, Simon! Satan, you must know, has got
32 his wish to sift you all like wheat; ·but I have
prayed for you, Simon, that your faith may not
fail, and once you have recovered, you in your
33 turn must strengthen your brothers." ·"Lord,"
he answered, "I would be ready to go to prison
34 with you, and to death." ·Jesus replied, "I tell you,
Peter, by the time the cock crows today you will
have denied three times that you know me."

35   He said to them, "When I sent you out without
purse or haversack or sandals, were you short of
36 anything? ·"No," they said. He said to them, "But
now if you have a purse, take it; if you have a
haversack, do the same; if you have no sword, sell
37 your cloak and buy one, ·because I tell you these
words of scripture have to be fulfilled in me: He
let himself be taken for a criminal. Yes, what
scripture says about me is even now reaching its
38 fulfillment." ·"Lord," they said, "there are two
swords here now." He said to them, "That is
enough!"

✠

When it comes to the events of Holy Week, I would
venture to say that all of us—myself included—suffer
from the disease of harmonizing-itis. That is, we har-
monize the events of those days, selecting bits and
pieces from each of the four Gospels—for example, the
footwashing scene from John, and Jesus' words to the
good thief from Luke. Unless we diagnose this disease
and take steps to combat it, we will miss much of what

is uniquely Luke's teaching in this section and in other parts of his passion account. I would suggest that one of the most effective remedies for harmonizing-itis is a big dose of active reading. Not just ordinary reading, during which we may tune in and out from time to time, but reading which is disciplined because we repeat in our own words what we think we have read. In the case at hand, this means that we can check the accuracy of what we think we have read by comparing it with the text and by contrasting it with the composite image of the Last Supper which harmonizing-itis has imprinted on our memory. Try this remedy; you'll like it.

If one were to ask what is unique about Luke's Last Supper, the answer would be: It's a series of short speeches. Given by Jesus on the eve of his death, these speeches embody his priceless legacy to his beloved. That legacy consists of the institution of the Eucharist, instructions on how to celebrate the Eucharist worthily, admonitions to church leaders who preside at the community's worship, and exhortations on how to cope with persecution. As Jesus speaks, his gaze is fixed on the future.

Jesus, knowing that he is about to die, ensures his continued presence with his community by means of the legacy of the Eucharist. This legacy is so rich that Luke devotes two accounts to it (22:14–18, and 19–20). These accounts are so streamlined and laced with symbolism that at a first reading their meaning can elude our grasp like mercury. Jesus and his beloved disciples are not eating a TV dinner or one picked up at a fast-food store like Colonel Sanders. It's a festive meal, like the ones we celebrate with toasts of wine or speeches to interpret the event. It begins as a passover meal whose symbolism recalls God's deliverance of the Jews from Egyptian slavery and points forward to God's future deliverance of his people.

Luke's first account highlights the meal as Jesus' meal *with his beloved* disciples (22:14–15). It is the culmination of those meals which Jesus shared with others as a sign of God's fellowship with them (see the commentary on 5:27–32). In verses 16 and 18 Jesus confidently looks forward to his future where he will enjoy the banquet of heaven. At that time the passover meal, which he now celebrates, will reach its fulfillment (22:16), for the future deliverance it points to will be present. Until that time, however, the cup which Jesus has blessed and which his beloved disciples have shared is a pledge of their participation with him at that eternal banquet (22:17). In brief, drinking the cup of the Eucharist is future-oriented, a foretaste of that final sharing with Jesus at the banquet which God has prepared for his beloved disciples.

The second account of the Eucharist clashes somewhat with the first. The symbolism of the passover meal, still present in the first account, recedes into the background. Jesus' legacy is a new meal with its own symbolism. This symbolism emerges in the bread which is broken and the wine which is poured out *for you* and points to the cross where Jesus' life is broken and his blood is poured out *for you*. The Eucharist points to and makes present the power of Jesus' death by which he atoned for sin. A further symbol is present in the words "new covenant." Covenant means God's pact or contract of love and mercy with his people. Israel frequently broke its covenant with God and longed for a new and lasting one. Jesus' death, symbolized by his blood, seals God's new covenant with his people. The Eucharist makes present God's new relationship with his people, a relationship effected by Jesus' death.

Now that Luke has depicted Jesus' Eucharistic legacy, he adapts the announcement of Judas' betrayal to
admonish communicants at the Lord's Supper. Note
that Judas' name is not mentioned in 22:21–23. This
is not a slip of Luke's pen. The disciples do not question Jesus about betrayal, but one another (contrast Mk
14:19). Luke looks beyond Jesus' Last Supper to his
own Lord's Supper and challenges the members of his
community to visualize themselves as Jesus' betrayers.
He asks, "Might you betray Jesus?" and suggests intra-
community scrutiny as a means of forestalling betrayal
of Jesus.

The fracas described in verses 24–27 is extraordinary
—a fight at the Last Supper! Luke could have used this
dispute in its Markan sequence (Mk 10:41–45) earlier
in his Gospel, but he elected to introduce and adapt
it here so that he could issue instructions for church
leaders who preside at Eucharist. They must remember
that the Eucharist makes Jesus the Servant present
among his beloved and should not be turned into a
power-grabbing charade. Church leaders and those who
preside at Eucharist must not ogle the fashionable leadership styles of their haughty pagan counterparts; their
leadership style must bear the label of Jesus the Servant.

Another legacy which Jesus leaves his church are
apostles whose task is to rule God's covenant people.
They are the new patriarchs who build up anew God's
people on the pattern of ancient Israel (22:29–30).
This glorious role does not render them immune from
participating in Jesus' trial of opposition and rejection.
Verse 28 underscores that factor in the life of church
leaders. They have stood by Jesus in the dangers of
his mission, dangers which will continue during the mission of the church.

The familiar figure of Simon Peter flashes on the screen (22:31–34). Luke does not give Peter a leading role to satisfy historical curiosity but to admonish his church in two regards. First, the Lord's intercessory prayer is so powerful that Peter's denial is not a loss of his faith in Jesus; it's an act of cowardice. Peter will repent of that cowardice, will be with Jesus at the crucifixion (see 23:49: "*All his friends* stood at a distance"), and will bear witness to Jesus (see Ac 1–5, where Peter is the prime witness to Jesus Christ). Christians celebrating Eucharist within Luke's community are in the presence of the same powerful Lord. Second, Luke exhorts the Peters within his own community to strengthen their Christian brethren, especially when they gather for Eucharist (22:32).

The final speech in this farewell discourse echoes two previous motifs in Luke's account of the Last Supper. Jesus' death is in accord with God's plan as revealed in the Scripture (22:37; see 22:22). The church of the future will suffer opposition and rejection like its Lord (22:35–38; see 22:28).

Luke stamps his account of the Last Supper with the imprint of his community's concerns. On the eve of his death Jesus does not abandon his beloved disciples, but bestows a precious legacy on them. As they battle danger after danger to remain faithful to Jesus, they are assured of his presence among them in the Eucharist.

STUDY QUESTIONS: Long years of experience and reflection stand behind the powerhouse theology of Eucharist present in this section. Why is the Eucharist so important for Luke? Is it possible for Christians today to recapture the depth of meaning

Luke perceived in Jesus' legacy of
the Lord's Supper? If today's Eucharistic celebrations are bland
and boring, is this due to the fact
that those who preside at them assume too much prominence?

Luke 22:39–53
A MARTYR'S PRAYER

39 He then left to make his way as usual to the Mount of Olives, with the disciples following.
40 When they reached the place he said to them, "Pray not to be put to the test."
41 Then he withdrew from them, about a stone's throw away, and knelt down and prayed.
42 "Father," he said, "if you are willing, take this cup away from me. Nevertheless, let your will be
43 done, not mine." ·Then an angel appeared to him,
44 coming from heaven to give him strength. ·In his anguish he prayed even more earnestly, and his sweat fell to the ground like great drops of blood.
45 When he rose from prayer he went to the disciples and found them sleeping for sheer grief.
46 "Why are you asleep?" he said to them. "Get up and pray not to be put to the test."
47 He was still speaking when a number of men appeared, and at the head of them the man called Judas, one of the Twelve, who went up to Jesus to
48 kiss him. ·Jesus said, "Judas, are you betraying the
49 Son of Man with a kiss?" ·His followers, seeing what was happening, said, "Lord, shall we use our
50 swords?" ·And one of them struck out at the high
51 priest's servant and cut off his right ear. ·But at this Jesus spoke. "Leave off!" he said. "That will do!" And touching the man's ear he healed him.
52 Then Jesus spoke to the chief priests and captains of the Temple guard and elders who had come for him. "Am I a brigand," he said, "that
53 you had to set out with swords and clubs? ·When I was among you in the Temple day after day you never moved to lay hands on me. But this is your hour; this is the reign of darkness."

✠

In this section Luke headlines Jesus, the Innocent Martyr, and gives lessons to members of his community who spy martyrdom around the corner.

Luke's account of Jesus on the mountain of prayer (22:39-46) has two unique features. First, Luke does not say that Jesus prayed three times as Matthew and Mark do. He centers all attention on Jesus' single prayer. Second, he brackets that prayer with the exhortation to all the disciples, "Pray not to be put to the test" (22:40, 46). Jesus' "anguish" in prayer (22:44) is not the result of being frightened senseless by the prospect of death. It can be likened to the "anguish" of a weight lifter trying to lift five hundred pounds. Jesus' "anguish" stems from the marshaling of all his strength and resolve to be obedient to his Father's will and to withstand the test of the crucifixion. Jesus at prayer is an example to his community as it faces the test of martyrdom. Luke exhorts his community to pray earnestly lest the test of martyrdom cause them to lose their faith. Such prayer to their Father will strengthen them as it did Jesus.

Luke 22:47-53 is the unfolding of the events set in motion by Judas (22:1-6). Unlike Matthew and Mark, Luke presents Jesus as a teacher who is in supreme command of the situation and is not seized until he ends his teaching (22:54). Since Jesus is not a political messiah, he will not sanction physical violence as a means of escaping from martyrdom—for himself or his followers (22:49-51). Jesus graphically illustrates that his mission is one of peace, not sword-wielding, by healing the servant's ear. There is not a single Roman soldier present in the crowd which comes to apprehend Jesus;

the Jewish religious authorities, and they alone, are responsible for Jesus' martyrdom (22:52). Since Jesus is innocent, they use night to cover their deed. Luke does not say that the apostles abandoned Jesus. All of them will be witnesses to his crucifixion; see 23:49: "*All his friends* stood at a distance." If the apostles had abandoned Jesus, they would not fit Luke's description of an apostle: "someone who was with us right from the time when John was baptizing until the day when he was taken up from us" (Ac 1:22).

STUDY QUESTION: Prayer and not the sword. Is this the American and Christian way of combatting oppression?

Luke 22:54–71
THE RESOLUTE AND MERCIFUL LORD

54 They seized him then and led him away, and they took him to the high priest's house. Peter
55 followed at a distance. ·They had lit a fire in the middle of the courtyard and Peter sat down
56 among them, ·and as he was sitting there by the blaze a servant girl saw him, peered at him, and
57 said, "This person was with him too." ·But he denied it. "Woman," he said, "I do not know
58 him." ·Shortly afterward someone else saw him and said, "You are another of them." But Peter
59 replied, "I am not, my friend." ·About an hour later another man insisted, saying, "This fellow was certainly with him. Why, he is a Galilean."
60 "My friend," said Peter, "I do not know what you are talking about." At that instant, while he was
61 still speaking, the cock crew, ·and the Lord turned and looked straight at Peter, and Peter remembered what the Lord had said to him, "Before the cock crows today, you will have disowned me
62 three times." ·And he went outside and wept bitterly.
63 Meanwhile the men who guarded Jesus were
64 mocking and beating him. ·They blindfolded him and questioned him. "Play the prophet," they
65 said. "Who hit you then?" ·And they continued heaping insults on him.
66 When day broke there was a meeting of the elders of the people, attended by the chief priests and scribes. He was brought before their council,
67 and they said to him, "If you are the Christ, tell us." "If I tell you," he replied, "you will not
68 believe me, ·and if I question you, you will not
69 answer. ·But from now on, the Son of Man will

be seated at the right hand of the Power of
70 God." •Then they all said, "So you are the Son of
God then?" He answered, "It is you who say I
71 am." •"What need of witnesses have we now?"
they said. "We have heard it for ourselves from
his own lips."

☩

This section contrasts Jesus' courageous stand before
the full panoply of Jewish authority (22:63–71) with
Peter's cowardly performance before such awesome figures as a maidservant (22:54–62). Luke addresses his
church which has to deal with members who cracked
during interrogation and groaned, "I don't know
Jesus!"

If you recall, Luke's Last Supper account contained
Jesus' assurance to Peter, "But I have prayed for you,
Simon, that your faith may not fail" (22:32). To show
that Peter's faith did not fail, Luke reinterprets the tradition of Peter's denials and does so in two ways. First,
a comparison with Mark 14:66–72 shows the extent to
which Luke has weakened the force of Peter's denials.
Peter's denials range from the weak "I do not know
what you are talking about" (Lk 22:60) to the mild
"I do not know him" (22:57). Luke omits the vehe-
mently strong denial which Mark has: "But he started
calling down curses on himself and swearing, 'I do not
know the man you speak of'" (Mk 14:71). Second,
it is Luke alone who has, "And the Lord turned and
looked straight at Peter" (22:61). The Lord's glance
of mercy and forgiveness causes Peter to shed copious
tears of repentance. For Luke, Peter's denials are a
grievous sin of cowardice, but not a loss of faith in
Jesus. Luke also uses this story to address a word of
challenge and consolation to the cowards of his com-

munity who have denied acquaintance with Jesus. The Lord directs a merciful glance toward them as he did toward Peter. Peter is their model.

Despite beatings and insults (22:63–65), Jesus is a rock before his accusers. By couching his answer to the Sanhedrin's question in religious categories, Jesus denies that he is a political messiah. Although they may reject him, God will vindicate him as Son of Man to assume the position of authority, symbolized by "right hand." Remember our common expression, "He's his right-hand man." The religious authorities see the implications of Jesus' answer and equate it with "Son of God."

In Luke the Sanhedrin does not accuse Jesus of blasphemy or pronounce a sentence of death. Luke streamlines his account of their "trial" to contrast Jesus' resoluteness with Peter's cowardice.

STUDY QUESTION: Can nonpersecuted churches, like those in the United States, still draw inspiration from the figure of the repentant Peter?

JESUS, THE INNOCENT MARTYR

¹ 23 The whole assembly then rose, and they brought him before Pilate.
² They began their accusation by saying, "We found this man inciting our people to revolt, opposing payment of the tribute to Caesar, and
³ claiming to be Christ, a king." ·Pilate put to him this question, "Are you the king of the Jews?"
⁴ "It is you who say it," he replied. ·Pilate then said to the chief priests and the crowd, "I find no case
⁵ against this man." ·But they persisted, "He is inflaming the people with his teaching all over Judaea; it has come all the way from Galilee,
⁶ where he started, down to here." ·When Pilate heard this, he asked if the man were a Galilean;
⁷ and finding that he came under Herod's jurisdiction he passed him over to Herod who was also in Jerusalem at that time.
⁸ Herod was delighted to see Jesus; he had heard about him and had been wanting for a long time to set eyes on him; moreover, he was hoping to see
⁹ some miracle worked by him. ·So he questioned him at some length; but without getting any reply.
¹⁰ Meanwhile the chief priests and the scribes were
¹¹ there, violently pressing their accusations. ·Then Herod, together with his guards, treated him with contempt and made fun of him; he put a rich
¹² cloak on him and sent him back to Pilate. ·And though Herod and Pilate had been enemies before, they were reconciled that same day.
¹³ Pilate then summoned the chief priests and the
¹⁴ leading men and the people. ·"You brought this man before me," he said, "as a political agitator. Now I have gone into the matter myself in your

presence and found no case against the man in respect of all the charges you bring against him.
15 Nor has Herod either, since he has sent him back to us. As you can see, the man has done nothing
16 that deserves death, ·so I shall have him flogged
18 and then let him go." ·But as one man they howled, "Away with him! Give us Barabbas!"
19 (This man had been thrown into prison for causing a riot in the city and for murder.)
20 Pilate was anxious to see Jesus free and ad-
21 dressed them again, ·but they shouted back,
22 "Crucify him! Crucify him!" ·And for the third time he spoke to them, "Why? What harm has this man done? I have found no case against him that deserves death, so I shall have him punished and
23 then let him go." ·But they kept on shouting at the top of their voices, demanding that he should be crucified. And their shouts were growing louder.
24 Pilate then gave his verdict: their demand was
25 to be granted. ·He released the man they asked for, who had been imprisoned for rioting and murder, and handed Jesus over to them to deal with as they pleased.

✠

In the general introduction to Luke 19:45 to 23:56 we gave a preview of several key themes in these chapters. The zoom lens of this section focuses on two of those themes: Jesus' innocence, and Jesus' rejection by the religious authorities.

The Sanhedrin is so intent on having Jesus killed that they go as one man to plead their case before Pilate. Their accusation is a tissue of lies and innuendo. When and where had Jesus incited the people to revolt against Roman rule? In his discussion about the tribute (20:20–26) had Jesus opposed payment of taxes to Roman authorities? In his trial before the Sanhedrin Jesus had in effect declared that he was not a political

messiah or king (22:66–71). Pilate is not taken in by
these trumped-up charges and conducts his own scrutiny. He quickly becomes an advocate for the defense:
"I find no case against this man" (23:4). The religious
authorities are not rebuffed by this finding and proceed
to Plan B of their strategy: Jesus, who comes from
Galilee—that hotbed of revolutionary activity—has been
radicalizing people all over Palestine with his seditious
tongue (23:5). Upon hearing of Jesus' Galilean origin,
Pilate seizes the opportunity of obtaining an outside
judgment on the case and sends Jesus off to Herod
Antipas.

After Jesus returns from Herod, Pilate regathers the
Jewish religious authorities and pronounces most solemnly that Jesus is innocent (23:14–15). The force of
Pilate's judgment is fully perceived once one realizes
the Old Testament background which Luke sees behind
it. In Deuteronomy 19:15 two witnesses are required
for a declaration of guilt or innocence. In the case at
hand, two witnesses, one a pagan and the other a Jew,
attest to Jesus' innocence. To cap Luke's argument, it
should be noted that Herod was Jesus' enemy (see
13:31). Even an enemy—hardly the person one would
expect to give impartial testimony—declares Jesus innocent.

All evidence to the contrary notwithstanding, the religious leaders continue to press for Jesus' death—by
crucifixion. They'll even tolerate a convicted murderer
loose on their streets before they'll let the innocent
Jesus go (23:19, 25). Pilate's third declaration of
Jesus' innocence falls on deaf ears (23:22). Under
pressure of mob action, he gives in to them. But Luke
makes it clear that Pilate did not deliver a guilty verdict
against Jesus: "Pilate then gave his verdict: their demand was to be granted. He . . . handed Jesus over

to them to deal with as they pleased" (23:24–25).
Jesus is innocent; he goes to his death a martyr.

Popular preaching has attuned us to see Luke's purpose written on the faces of the principal characters in
this section: Don't imitate Pilate's expediency; don't be
a thrill-seeking Herod; your heart can be hardened like
that of the religious leaders. No doubt, such hortatory
displays capture part of Luke's purpose. Yet Luke's intent runs deeper and is apologetic. Even though their
opponents may charge them with sedition, Christians
are no more revolutionary than Jesus, their Lord. And
the Roman officials should and do realize this. There
is a further side to Luke's intent. Earlier in his Gospel
(12:11–12 and 21:12–14) Luke consoled his persecuted community with the promise that the Lord would
provide their defense attorney. This section goes beyond the trial scene of persecuted Christians and conveys a message of stark realism: Although innocent of
the charges of sedition, Christians in Luke's church may
be given over to the will of their opponents. As in the
case of Jesus the martyr, their innocence will be vindicated by God.

STUDY QUESTION: Is Luke's goal in this section to
write history?

THE LAST WORDS TELL THE STORY

26   As they were leading him away they seized on a
man, Simon from Cyrene, who was coming in
from the country, and made him shoulder the
27 cross and carry it behind Jesus. ·Large numbers of
people followed him, and of women too, who
28 mourned and lamented for him. ·But Jesus turned
to them and said, "Daughters of Jerusalem, do
not weep for me; weep rather for yourselves and
29 for your children. ·For the days will surely come
when people will say, 'Happy are those who are
barren, the wombs that have never borne, the
30 breasts that have never suckled!' ·Then they will
begin to say to the mountains, 'Fall on us!'; to the
31 hills, 'Cover us!' ·For if men use the green wood
32 like this, what will happen when it is dry?" ·Now
with him they were also leading out two other
criminals to be executed.

33   When they reached the place called The Skull,
they crucified him there and the two criminals
34 also, one on the right, the other on the left. ·Jesus
said, "Father, forgive them; they do not know
what they are doing." Then they cast lots to share
out his clothing.

35   The people stayed there watching him. As for
the leaders, they jeered at him. "He saved others,"
they said, "let him save himself if he is the Christ
36 of God, the Chosen One." ·The soldiers mocked
him too, and when they approached to offer him
37 vinegar ·they said, "If you are the king of the
38 Jews, save yourself." ·Above him there was an inscription: "This is the King of the Jews."

39   One of the criminals hanging there abused him.
"Are you not the Christ?" he said. "Save yourself

40 and us as well." ·But the other spoke up and rebuked him. "Have you no fear of God at all?"
he said. "You got the same sentence as he did,
41 but in our case we deserved it: we are paying
for what we did. But this man has done nothing
42 wrong. ·Jesus," he said, "remember me when you
43 come into your kingdom." ·"Indeed, I promise
you," he replied, "today you will be with me in
paradise."

44   It was now about the sixth hour and, with the
sun eclipsed, a darkness came over the whole land
45 until the ninth hour. ·The veil of the Temple was
46 torn right down the middle; ·and when Jesus had
cried out in a loud voice, he said, "Father, into
your hands I commit my spirit." With these words
he breathed his last.

47   When the centurion saw what had taken place,
he gave praise to God and said, "This was a great
48 and good man." ·And when all the people who
had gathered for the spectacle saw what had happened, they went home beating their breasts.

49   All his friends stood at a distance; so also did
the women who had accompanied him from Galilee, and they saw all this happen.

50   Then a member of the council arrived, an up-
51 right and virtuous man named Joseph. ·He had
not consented to what the others had planned
and carried out. He came from Arimathaea, a
Jewish town, and he lived in the hope of seeing
52 the kingdom of God. ·This man went to Pilate
53 and asked for the body of Jesus. ·He then took it
down, wrapped it in a shroud and put him in a
tomb which was hewn in stone in which no one
54 had yet been laid. ·It was Preparation Day and
the sabbath was imminent.

55   Meanwhile the women who had come from
Galilee with Jesus were following behind. They
took note of the tomb and of the position of the
body.

56   Then they returned and prepared spices and
ointments. And on the sabbath day they rested,
as the Law required.

✠

When I was a boy, the most popular Good Friday devotion was the *Tre Ore* service with its sermons on Jesus' last words. Although this devotion is out of vogue today, it had its finger on the pulse of the Gospel accounts of Jesus' crucifixion. We will center our comments on Jesus' last words—the heart of this section (23:28–31, 34, 43, 46).

Luke provides a theological lead-in for each of Jesus' last words. For his lead-in to Jesus' first word, he adds "and carry it behind Jesus" to Mark's description of Simon of Cyrene's cross-bearing and thus makes Simon a model for Christians who follow in Jesus' footsteps (23:26). Jesus' first word is a prophecy, foretelling the destruction of Jerusalem, akin to the one which he uttered as he approached the Holy City for the last time (19:41–44). Because the Jewish religious leaders rejected God's Son and prophet, their Temple and Holy City will be devastated. Jesus cautions the women not to be concerned about him, but about themselves. For if men treat the green wood—the innocent Jesus—like this, what will happen when it comes to dry wood—the unrepentant sinners?

Jesus' innocence is the setting for his second word. It is out of theological conviction and not for stylistic variation that Luke separates Jesus the innocent one from the two criminals: "They crucified him there and the two criminals also" (23:33). Jesus' second word is a powerful summary of his entire mission: "Father, forgive them; they do not know what they are doing" (23:34). It is also the hallmark of Jesus the Martyr, who does not rail against his murderers. Jesus' conduct was not lost on later Christian martyrs. In a parallel passage Luke describes the death of the martyr Stephen: "Then he knelt down and said aloud, 'Lord, do not hold this sin against them'" (Ac 7:60).

The lead-in to Jesus' third word is long and replete with Lukan themes (23:35–42). As we have had frequent occasion to note, Luke distances the people of God from their leaders (23:35). It is these leaders who mock and jeer at Jesus while the people stand by watching. The jeers of the Jewish religious leaders, the Roman soldiers, and the one criminal mask the genuine Christian message. Jesus is indeed the Christ of God, the Chosen One, the King of the Jews. He has saved others. But Jesus, faithful to his Father's will to the end, will not use his power to feather his own nest. Earlier, Pilate and Herod had witnessed to Jesus' innocence. Now the "good criminal" adds his independent witness: "But this man has done nothing wrong" (23:41). The jewel in this rich setting of theological themes follows. It is Jesus' third word, sometimes called the Gospel within the Gospel: "Indeed, I promise you, today you will be with me in paradise" (23:43). Jesus had come to put his arms of mercy around sinners and hug them. To the very last he is true to that kingly vocation. The "good revolutionary" is promised salvation today, not in some dim future. The words "with me" and "in paradise" mean the same thing: The sinner will enjoy communion with Jesus after his death. The clear implications of Jesus' promise are that his death and exaltation to glory at the Father's right hand occur at the same time. Because Jesus will enjoy that blissful state today, he can promise a share of it to the criminal.

Luke's theological introduction to Jesus' last word zeroes in on the profound significance which Jesus' death has for Jewish worship. The tearing asunder of the veil of the Temple (23:45) is just the first stage in the destruction of the Temple itself. Entry to God's presence is no longer through the veil of the Temple, but through Jesus' death. In calm confidence Jesus utters his last word. He does not die with a curse against God on his lips nor in anguished confusion over his destiny. He serenely commits his life to his Father, in whom he had put all his trust (23:46).

The events which follow Jesus' last words and death are like the comments of analysts who weigh the meaning of major political speeches. The first analyst is the centurion, who perceives God at work in Jesus' last words and death and praises God. His declaration, "This was a great and good man," adds still another witness for Jesus' innocence (23:47). The people who beat their breasts as a sign of their repentance, Jesus' friends (his apostles), and the faithful women (23:48–49) comment on the significance of Jesus' last words and death by becoming the first members of his church (see Ac 1 and 2). Joseph of Arimathaea wraps up the analysts' remarks by witnessing to the innocence of Jesus the martyr (23:51).

If the last words of any person carry precious freight for their loved ones, how much more those of Jesus the Christ! Perhaps the most important word for members of Luke's community is Jesus' third: "Indeed, I promise you, today you will be with me in paradise." As they shoulder Jesus' cross and are marched to martyrdom, they are assured that death is not going to spit in their faces. The martyred Jesus is their Lord who saves beyond death.

STUDY QUESTIONS: Jesus' last words confront us with the hard question: "And you, who do you say that I am?" Does

Luke's account of Jesus' last words accord with our image of Jesus? Does the picture of Jesus the Martyr have any relevance for Christians today?

The End of the Jesus Story
Is Just a Beginning
Luke 24:1–53

THE END OF THE JESUS STORY
IS JUST A BEGINNING

1 24 On the first day of the week, at the first sign of dawn, they went to the tomb with 2 the spices they had prepared. ·They found that the stone had been rolled away from the tomb, 3 but on entering discovered that the body of the 4 Lord Jesus was not there. ·As they stood there not knowing what to think, two men in brilliant 5 clothes suddenly appeared at their side. ·Terrified, the women lowered their eyes. But the two men said to them, "Why look among the dead for 6 someone who is alive? ·He is not here; he has risen. Remember what he told you when he was 7 still in Galilee: ·that the Son of Man had to be handed over into the power of sinful men and be crucified, and rise again on the third day." 8 And they remembered his words.

9 When the women returned from the tomb they told all this to the Eleven and to all the others. 10 The women were Mary of Magdala, Joanna, and Mary the mother of James. The other women 11 with them also told the apostles, ·but this story of theirs seemed pure nonsense, and they did not believe them.

12 Peter, however, went running to the tomb. He bent down and saw the binding cloths but nothing else; he then went back home, amazed at what had happened.

13 That very same day, two of them were on their way to a village called Emmaus, seven miles from 14 Jerusalem, ·and they were talking together about 15 all that had happened. ·Now as they talked this over, Jesus himself came up and walked by their

16 side; ·but something prevented them from recog-
17 nizing him. ·He said to them, "What matters are
you discussing as you walk along?" They stopped
short, their faces downcast.

18 Then one of them, called Cleopas, answered
him, "You must be the only person staying in
Jerusalem who does not know the things that have
19 been happening there these last few days." ·"What
things?" he asked. "All about Jesus of Nazareth,"
they answered, "who proved he was a great
prophet by the things he said and did in the sight
20 of God and of the whole people; ·and how our
chief priests and our leaders handed him over to
21 be sentenced to death, and had him crucified. ·Our
own hope had been that he would be the one to
set Israel free. And this is not all: two whole days
22 have gone by since it all happened; ·and some
women from our group have astounded us: they
23 went to the tomb in the early morning, ·and when
they did not find the body, they came back to tell
us they had seen a vision of angels who declared
24 he was alive. ·Some of our friends went to the
tomb and found everything exactly as the women
had reported, but of him they saw nothing."

25 Then he said to them, "You foolish men! So
slow to believe the full message of the prophets!
26 Was it not ordained that the Christ should suffer
27 and so enter into his glory?" ·Then, starting with
Moses and going through all the prophets, he explained to them the passages throughout the scriptures that were about himself.

28 When they drew near to the village to which
29 they were going, he made as if to go on; ·but they
pressed him to stay with them. "It is nearly evening," they said, "and the day is almost over."
30 So he went in to stay with them. ·Now while he
was with them at table, he took the bread and
said the blessing; then he broke it and handed it
31 to them. ·And their eyes were opened and they
recognized him; but he had vanished from their
32 sight. ·Then they said to each other, "Did not our

hearts burn within us as he talked to us on the road and explained the scriptures to us?"

33 They set out that instant and returned to Jerusalem. There they found the Eleven assembled to-
34 gether with their companions, ·who said to them, "Yes, it is true. The Lord has risen and has ap-
35 peared to Simon." ·Then they told their story of what had happened on the road and how they had recognized him at the breaking of bread.

36 They were still talking about all this when he himself stood among them and said to them,
37 "Peace be with you!" ·In a state of alarm and fright, they thought they were seeing a ghost.
38 But he said, "Why are you so agitated, and why
39 are these doubts rising in your hearts? ·Look at my hands and feet; yes, it is I indeed. Touch me and see for yourselves; a ghost has no flesh and
40 bones as you can see I have." ·And as he said this
41 he showed them his hands and feet. ·Their joy was so great that they still could not believe it, and they stood there dumfounded; so he said to
42 them, "Have you anything here to eat?" ·And
43 they offered him a piece of grilled fish, ·which he took and ate before their eyes.

44 Then he told them, "This is what I meant when I said, while I was still with you, that everything written about me in the Law of Moses, in the Prophets and in the Psalms, has to be fulfilled."
45 He then opened their minds to understand the
46 scriptures, ·and he said to them, "So you see how it is written that the Christ would suffer and on
47 the third day rise from the dead, ·and that, in his name, repentance for the forgiveness of sins would be preached to all the nations, beginning
48 from Jerusalem. ·You are witnesses to this.

49 "And now I am sending down to you what the Father has promised. Stay in the city then, until you are clothed with the power from on high."
50 Then he took them out as far as the outskirts of Bethany, and lifting up his hands he blessed
51 them. ·Now as he blessed them, he withdrew from

⁵² them and was carried up to heaven. ·They wor-
shiped him and then went back to Jerusalem full
⁵³ of joy; ·and they were continually in the Temple
praising God.

✠

We come to the end of Luke's Gospel. Accustomed
as we are to the events of the first Easter Day, we may
miss the startling character of Luke's final chapter.
Don't stories about a great man of the past, say a Jef-
ferson or Lincoln, conclude with the narration of his
death? Oh, perhaps there's a word or two about his
legacy, but then the curtain is drawn. Surprisingly,
though, Luke's story does not end with Jesus' death.
Jesus is alive! God has resurrected him. Let's use three
images to open the door to Luke's message in this final
section: the concluding chapter of a book, the execu-
tion of the leader of a movement, and a captivatingly
beautiful quilt.

Although it's been some ten years ago, I can still recall the powerful emotions which pulsed through me
when I finished reading John Steinbeck's *The Grapes
of Wrath*. Its last chapter harnessed all the themes of
the book into one overwhelming image, that of a nurs-
ing mother giving suckle and life to a starving adult.
This example of the summarizing character of a book's
last chapter leads us down the road to appreciating
Luke's achievement in chapter 24, where he captures
the cascading waters of his themes in a single figure,
that of the Risen Lord Jesus.

The Gospel commenced with the priest Zechariah in
the Temple and hit its story-line stride in its central section with Jesus' journey to the Temple. Now it ends
with Jesus' disciples continually in the Temple praising
God and with the blessing of the priest, the Risen Lord

Jesus, who has just completed the liturgy of his life
(24:50–51). All through the Gospel there have been
murmurings of doubt about Jesus and his mission. Similar mutterings course through this final chapter
(24:11, 12, 17, 25–26, 37, 41). But for the first and
only time in the Gospel, doubt gives way to worship
as the disciples worship the Risen Lord Jesus (24:52).
During his ministry Jesus had gathered disciples as witnesses. Now they are poised on the brink of their mission of witnessing to God's Risen Son, Jesus (24:48).
These are the most important themes which cluster
around the recapitulating image of the Risen Lord
Jesus.

The image of the last chapter of a book provides still
another key to chapter 24. Imagine the Sherlock
Holmes buffs who reach the end of another thriller. As
they revel in the mastery by which their hero has put
all the pieces of the mystery puzzle together, they look
forward to tagging along with him on his next case.
Luke, too, leaves his readers leaning forward with keen
anticipation to his next volume. In 24:44–53 his story
does not trail off with the solution to the murder of
Jesus, but points forward to his next book, The Acts
of the Apostles, and its story of the missionary work
of the church of Jesus the Messiah. Jesus' new community will be formed in God's Holy City, Jerusalem,
to show that it, as the people of God, is heir to God's
promises to Israel (24:49). From Jerusalem the gospel
will be preached to all the nations (24:47). The script
writer for much of Luke's sequel to his gospel will be
Jesus' Spirit who will guide the new community in its
continuation of Jesus' mission (24:49).

Another image can give us good directions to Luke's
message in chapter 24. Recall how frequently govern-
ments squelch a movement by arresting or executing its

leader. Without its leader the movement loses heart and withers away. Behind Luke's account of the events of that first Easter day we can see the heart going out of Jesus' disciples as they muse: "It's all over now. He's dead. We had a good thing going and then. . . . Was Jesus really God's prophet? Why should we struggle to follow his teachings? Maybe our religious leaders were right after all in condemning him to death?" Furthest from their minds was any notion that God would vindicate their leader by raising him from the dead. The women's tale that Jesus was alive was utter nonsense. The empty tomb may be a mystery for now, but it can be explained. Just give us time. The Jesus movement thrashes wildly in its death throes. See how easy it is to defuse a movement by liquidating its leader.

The wonder, grandeur, and mystery of Easter is that Jesus has not been liquidated. He is alive and has appeared to Simon Peter. The two disciples on the way to Emmaus have encountered him in the breaking of bread. He has appeared to the Eleven and their companions, shown them his hands and feet, and even eaten a piece of grilled fish. Jesus, the innocent martyr, is not vindicated like an executed criminal whose innocence is later proven by the discovery of new evidence. Whereas that new verdict of innocence will not bring the dead man back to life, God has declared Jesus innocent and given him life. He's not a resuscitated corpse like Lazarus, who will die at some future time. Transformed by the power of God, his body is alive with God's life. Yet his disciples are able to identify the Risen Lord with Jesus of Nazareth. Through God's gift of the resurrection Jesus shares God's powers. He has authority to grace his disciples with the largess of the promised Holy Spirit. Because of Jesus those who accept the preaching of his disciples will have their sins forgiven. Jesus is worthy of the worship due God alone. Yes, Jesus is very much alive. His appearances to his disciples instill new heart and life into them. They aren't sure what God has in store for them, but their Father, who would not let his faithful Son Jesus suffer the corruption of death, is surely to be trusted—no matter how obscure and troubled the future may be.

A final image will illumine Luke's message from still another angle. A friend of mine has an exquisitely wrought quilt. While the individual pieces are the work of various women, the completed quilt owes its beauty to the masterful skills of the artist who sewed the individual pieces together to create the quilt's magnificent array of colors and patterns. In many respects this chapter resembles that superbly crafted quilt. Other Christians have worked on the traditions which Luke has assembled in chapter 24. In themselves these traditions are of different hues and shapes: the story of the empty tomb (24:1–11), Peter's visit to the tomb (24:12), the story of the disciples on the way to Emmaus (24:13–33, 35), the announcement that the Lord has risen and appeared to Simon (24:34), the story of Jesus' appearance to the Eleven and their companions (24:36–43). Behind each stands a skilled artist. But it is due to the creative genius of Luke that they form the beautifully moving conclusion to the third Gospel.

As you run your finger and eye over chapter 24, you can detect one of the weaves which Luke used to create this chapter—fulfillment of promise:

"Remember what he told you when he was still in Galilee: that the Son of Man had to be handed over into the power of sinful men and be crucified, and rise again on the third day" (24:6–7).

" 'You foolish men! So slow to believe the full message of the prophets! Was it not ordained that the Christ should suffer and so enter into his glory?' Then, starting with Moses and going through all the prophets, he explained to them the passages throughout the scriptures that were about himself" (24:25–27).

" 'This is what I meant when I said, while I was still with you, that everything written about me in the Law of Moses, in the Prophets and in the Psalms, has to be fulfilled.' He then opened their minds to understand the scriptures . . ." (24:44–45).

Perplexed and terrified women, despondent travelers to Emmaus, and dumfounded disciples are given the same insight into the mystery of Jesus' death and resurrection: These events are the fulfillment of promise. Foretold in the Scriptures long ago, these events have now come to pass. The Risen Lord Jesus is proof positive that God is faithful to his promises; he did not let his faithful one, Jesus, suffer corruption. By means of this weave Luke underlines God's control over the events of salvation and his fidelity to his promises. Yet Luke's glance is not so much fixed on the past of God's fidelity as it is on the future of Jesus' church. Contemplating God's fidelity to his promises to Jesus, Jesus' church can gain confidence in the Father who has promised to be with them as they continue the Messiah's mission in troubled times (24:49).

Besides the issue of God's fidelity, Luke reflects other concerns of his church in his masterful chapter 24. To supply ammunition against those critics who might carp that the disciples fabricated the message of Jesus' resurrection, Luke rejoins that the disciples, caught in the vortex of disillusionment, were anything but eager to believe the message themselves. It took the appearances of the Risen Lord and his explanation of God's plan for him in the Scriptures to convince them that he was the Risen Messiah. To those Christians who despise the body as unworthy of God's life, Luke insists that the Risen Jesus is not a ghost (24:39). Jesus' full humanity —his earthly body included—has been infused with the new life of the resurrection. Thus, despite the scandal it might cause among his body-scorning readers, Luke must champion the point that the redemption promised to those who follow Jesus is not limited to their spiritual element but embraces their entire human person. In the artistic story of the disciples on their way to Emmaus, Jesus' homily on the meaning of Scripture and his breaking of bread capture the spotlight. While the Ascension may mark the end of Jesus' life on earth, it does not spell the absence of the Risen Lord from his church. He is present to them in word and meal. But to recognize his presence, the church must invite him to sup. Only then will he become their host and give them life.

When all is said and done, the meaning of Jesus' resurrection remains a mystery which eludes our grasp. Pondering its meaning through images is extremely helpful, but is like viewing a precious Rembrandt painting through venetian blinds. Flashes of insight and appreciation must substitute for total comprehension. Perhaps the ancient Introit for the Easter morning Mass put it most simply and profoundly: "I am risen, and am still with you."

STUDY QUESTIONS: Does the fact of an empty tomb supply any evidence for Jesus' resurrection? What does Jesus' resurrection say about the value of God's material creation? How and where does one encounter the Risen Lord Jesus today?

SUGGESTED FURTHER READINGS

Caird, G. B. *The Gospel of St Luke*. Pelican Gospel Commentaries. Baltimore: Penguin Books, 1963. Paper. In this concise commentary Caird sees a persecution situation as the occasion for the writing of the Gospel.

Danker, Frederick W. *Jesus and the New Age According to St. Luke: A Commentary on the Third Gospel*. St. Louis: Clayton Publishing House, 1972. Paper. Brims with contemporary applications of Luke's Gospel.

———. *Luke*. Proclamation Commentaries. Philadelphia: Fortress Press, 1976. Paper. The first draft of a blueprint for future study on Luke's Gospel.

Ellis, E. Earle. *The Gospel of Luke*. 2nd ed. Century Bible. London: Oliphants, 1975. Perhaps the most authoritative English commentary on Luke's Gospel today.

Karris, Robert J. *Gospel of St. Luke*. Read and Pray. Chicago: Franciscan Herald, 1974. Paper. Brief comments, reflections, and prayers invite the reader to pray the Gospel.

Morris, Leon. *The Gospel According to St. Luke: An Introduction and Commentary*. Tyndale New Testament Commentaries. Grand Rapids: Eerdmans, 1974. Paper. Focuses on Luke the historian who hands on the authentic Jesus story.

Senior, Donald. *Jesus: A Gospel Portrait*. Dayton: Pflaum, 1975. Paper. A highly readable and faith-filled study of what the four Gospels tell us about Jesus of Nazareth.

Talbert, Charles H. "Shifting Sands: The Recent Study of the Gospel of Luke," *Interpretation* 30 (1976), 381–95. This periodical article is a very reliable guide to the current state of scholarly research on Luke's Gospel.

S37